365 SEX THRILLS

Text, design, and concept copyright © 2013 Ulysses Press. Photos copyright © 2009 Hollan Publishing, Inc. All rights reserved. Any unauthorized duplication in whole or in part or dissemination of this edition by any means (including but not limited to photocopying, electronic devices, digital versions, and the internet) will be prosecuted to the fullest extent of the law.

Published by: AMORATA PRESS,
    an imprint of Ulysses Press
    PO Box 3440
    Berkeley, CA 94703
    www.ulyssespress.com

ISBN: 978-1-61243-112-3
Library of Congress Control Number: 2012909491

10 9 8 7 6 5 4 3 2 1

Acquisitions Editor: Keith Riegert
Managing Editor: Claire Chun
Editor: Paula Dragosh
Proofreader: Barbara Shultz
Design and layout: Wade Nights
Production: Jake Flaherty
Photographs: Hollan Publishing, Inc.

365 SEX THRILLS

Positions, Tricks and Techniques for an Erotic Year

Lisa Sweet

Amorata Press

LA CAGE AUX FOLLES

The tight maneuvering of this pose means she can grind her bottom against his groin while he's inside her, massaging parts of his rod that normally don't get a lot of action—and incidentally giving her own G-spot a naughty nudge at the same time.

2 BLIND MAN'S BLUFF

The titillating anonymity that comes with wearing masks during playtime means that everything is up for grabs and anything goes.

OEUFS DE L'EXTASE 3

These vibrators may be small, but they pack a powerful punch that will have her cock-a-doodling in seconds flat. That's a good thing, since high-intensity vibrations can make the holder's hand numb after prolonged use.

4 BEGGING FOR MORE

This is a high-potency pose, so using shallow thrusts and deep breathing will help him last longer—then again, if he's getting tired raising her up, they can wham and go bam quickly.

THE PINNER | 5

Lifting and lightly holding her legs up lets him spread her cheeks apart and go even deeper into her dark side.

6 TAKE IT OFF

A great strip is all in the accessories—wearing an outfit that's easy to remove but has lots of things to play with like zippers, buttons, ribbon ties, and buckles helps build anticipation to heady heights.

SPACE SHUTTLE 7

The only thing that's easy for her in this upside-down pose is the reverse angle because it means she can deep-throat him without gagging. Since this will, luckily, move things along quickly, she can pace her own pleasure to match his.

8 INTIMATE THINGS

It may feel like sexy lingerie is a waste of money and effort, since it's going to end up on the floor in a few minutes anyway, but a peek-a-boo bra-and-underwear set are made to be left on while guaranteeing he won't be able to keep his hands off her.

HELPING HAND

It isn't easy for her to fondle their naughty bits while standing, but a girl's gotta do what a girl's gotta do—especially if his hands are otherwise pleasurably occupied.

10 BELLY UP

Her belly and love bump are surprisingly similar in that they're made from the same blissful tissue. When he dips his tongue into her navel, it may feel like he's delving right into her nether regions.

CHILL THRILL 11

A cold front can turn up the heat during a blow job. To make him really sweat, though, she can alternate between lightly rubbing an ice cube over his shaft and taking him in her mouth.

12 MÉNAGE À TWO AND A HALF

Bringing a Fleshlight into bed is like adding a second very hot, experienced woman to the love play—especially since some are molded from the bodies of popular porn stars.

SOAP ON A ROPE | 13

This move stands and delivers. He's in charge of balance, so he should set the pace—at least initially. The more she arches her back, the more thoroughly he'll be giving her an inner scrubdown.

14 FINGER KISS

He can prime her for a swoony take-me-now smooch by first lightly caressing her lips with barely-there strokes while gazing deep into her eyes.

HANDY 69 | 15

While 69 sounds decadently good in theory (have your cake and eat it!), it can be difficult to put in play. But since the pose also allows complete access to his and her moan zones, lovers can take turns taking a break from tongue play to give a rear end massage, using strong and regular strokes that match each other's rhythm.

16 THE RECLINING CHAIR

This may look like an everyday woman-on-top position, but it comes with an intense climax slant. It gives her complete control of the rhythm and speed, and her body angle means he'll stimulate her G-spot directly. To switch the sensation, she can lean forward and grind her pelvis so that he's now stirring up her clit.

THRUSTERS 17

Sexercises like this aren't just a hot way to get fit—turns out that getting the heart rate up is a hot and heavy aphrodisiac, setting lovers up for a superstrength orgasm.

18 FREESTYLE

This is an open-and-shut pose where she gives him a little love squeeze on every upward stroke. The extra friction will have him doing record-breaking orgasmic laps in no time.

PLAY BALL 19

She'll make him go ballistic—in a good way—
by reaching around and giving his balls a
little tickle with her fingertips midplay.

20 TOE JOB

Toe fellatio doesn't exactly have a sexy ring to it, but it can have the same erotic effect as lavishing some lip love on his more well-known sexual appendage.

LOVE AT FIRST BITE | 21

Gentle biting brings blood to the surface of the skin, making it more sensitive to touch. She can tap into her inner vampire by first gently tugging the thin skin around his neck with her teeth and then sucking.

22 | CARNAL FEAST

She can satisfy all her red-hot desires by placing her feet on the sides of the chair and pausing at the end of each thrust to rub against him before pushing in again.

TEASING TOUCHES | 23

True, his tool requires lots of hands-on stimulation, but she can really dazzle him by mixing up her touchy-feely moves with a rough and then gentle approach, squeezing and then stroking lightly, gripping him with her entire palm and then tantalizingly trailing her fingers . . . he won't know which way to squirm.

24 BEST BJ

This pose gives a wide range of motion and plenty of access to his package without strain, but she should look up and make eye contact now and then to keep the connection above the belt.

HIGH FIVE | 25

The hands are so often used as love tools that it's easy to forget that giving them a little stimulation can be a pleasure trip in itself.

26 HER MISSION

Classic missionary is a somewhat difficult position for the woman to move freely, especially if the man is much larger than she is. Here she can control his penetration by flexing her thighs.

TOMCAT 27

This tried-and-true method will drive her to ecstasy: He starts with the vibrator at its lowest speed, increasing the intensity slowly until it's running at full throttle to get blood flowing to the clit and labia. At her point of no return, he shifts gears down, then cranks them back up again. Repeat until she crashes.

28 NEGLIGENT FOREPLAY

To turn him on just a bit more, she can let one sleeve of her slip do just that—slip—to reveal her touchable curves. He won't be able to stop himself from reaching for more.

PRESSURE POINTS 29

His bottom area is chockablock with tingly nerves that connect straight to his hot rod. She can power-drive his carnal chakras by pushing on the O-shaped knob at the base of his spine and then moving her hands lower until she's pressing her fingertips into the outer crease of each cheek before slowly dragging her fingers together.

30 THE SPHINX

The pressure of his body pressing up and down against her back will bend the dangle of his angle in new ways, making this powerfully pleasurable for both of them.

HEAD HONCHO 31

A well-executed desk move, it allows him to multitask on her body so he can get his entire To Do to Her Now list done before it's time to clock out.

32 A TOUCH OF GLASS

He'll cast an orgasmic spell over her by adding a glass wand to his bag of magic tricks. Using the dildo to glide and slide rather than plunge is sure to completely bewitch her—especially if he pops it in a glass of hot or ice-cold water first.

SPLITTING THE BAMBOO | 33

To get a dead center hit on her G-spot, she can try switching her legs—for some women, it's left leg up and right leg down that connects with this moan zone.

34 HURTS SO GOOD

The delicate pucker of the anus is packed with sensitive nerve endings, so all it takes is a tiny taste to push her over the ecstasy edge.

VA-VA-VOOM | 35

When missionary begins to feel like the same-old, she can give it a vixenish twist with a leg-raising V. As he enters, she can lift her hips up slightly to create a tighter fit for his vigorous thrusts.

36 RAMP IT UP

Adding a slight tilt to a classic 69 position angles the action so that it's easier for both partners to be in control of getting and giving pleasure at the same time.

FEED YOUR FACE | 37

This is a tricky pose for her to hold for long, but the spot-on pleasure she will get makes it oh!-oh!-oh!-so-worth-it.

38 WASH BEHIND THE EARS

She can take advantage of the clean and fresh effect of shower sex by dropping to her knees and pleasing him. The water will keep things slick, but she should remember to come up for air so she doesn't drown!

REVERSE SPOON | 39

The head-to-toe turnaround makes up for height differences that can sometimes hinder sideways positions—while opening up all sorts of other arousing opportunities.

40 TREASURE CHEST

Guys like having some TLC (tender lip care) given to their chest, too, but she should resist the urge to head straight for the nipples and instead build momentum by licking and kissing the entire area in semicircular swirls.

BLISS BUTTONS 41

She shouldn't be shy about womanhandling his nipples—this part of his body is so often overlooked, and all it takes is a tantalizing touch to trigger shock waves of pleasure.

42 BELLY BUDDHA

A woman's tummy is a place many men don't dare go, but the area between her belly button and pubic bone is actually packed with pleasure points. To arouse them all, he can place one hand palm down over her belly button and the other hand palm up between her breasts and gently press.

SOUTH SEAS ROCK | 43

Not to be attempted by the balance-challenged, this variation of a straightforward squat requires her to keep her legs closer together. This will create some fabulous friction but may also cause her to tip over—which might be embarrassing for her, but will most definitely be painful for him!

44 LITTLE MINX

Getting into character by slipping into a cute little outfit is a huge turn-on for him. He'll give extra carnal credit if she lets him play passion professor.

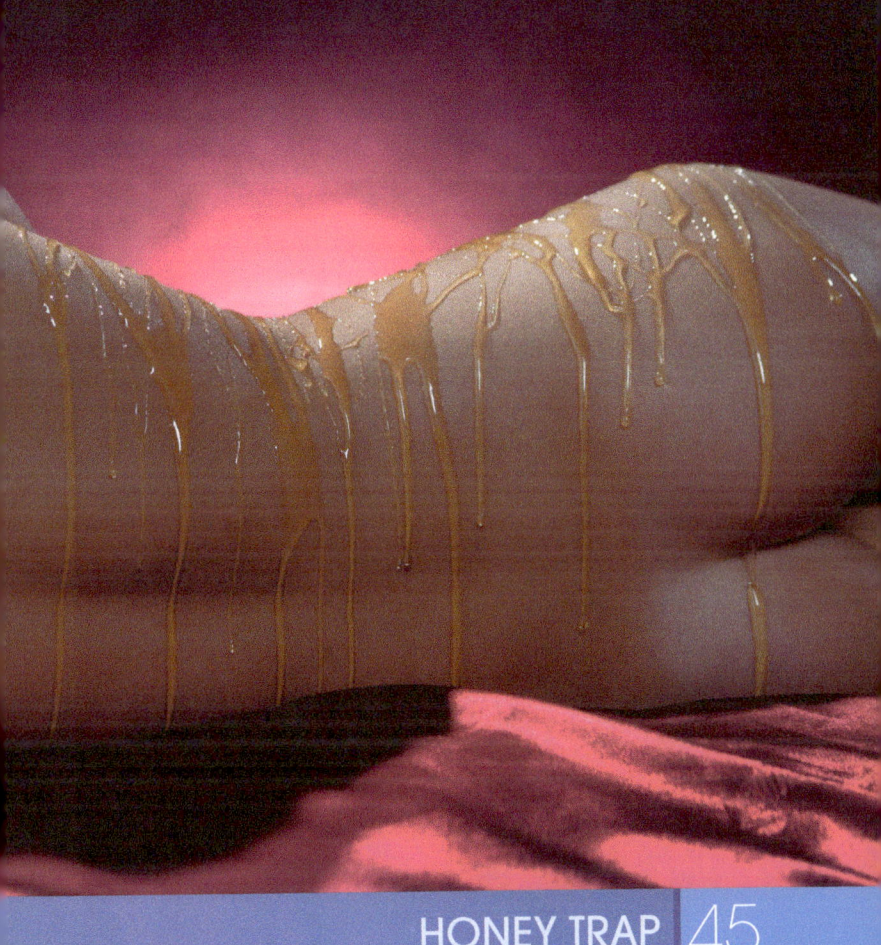

HONEY TRAP | 45

Dribbling honey over each other's bodies will add a sweet, sticky touch to lovemaking. One tasty trick to try is for him to spread it over her labia and then have her kneel above him to let it drip onto his lips.

46 | BITE IT

The big toe is considered an express route to awakening carnal cravings, so any kind of nip is going to whet the appetite.

BENDY SPOON | 47

Unlike regular spoon, the unique angle adds a couple of extra inches to his thrusts, allowing for deeper penetration.

48 A THOUSAND KISSES

Oral sex is so comfortable for him in this position that he'll want to tame his tongue and take it slow and soft, teasing her with sensual kisses as he builds her up to an extreme orgasm. Chances are she'll want to return the favor.

THE WINDSOR 49

Getting tied up instantly intensifies the sexual energy because it puts her at the mercy of his urges yet gives her the freedom to completely focus on her own pleasure. And vice versa!

50 TIC TOC, TIC TOC

Transform an ordinary kitchen timer into a sex toy: Lovers take turns challenging each other to get them off in a set time. When the ringer sounds, time's up and, if so inclined, they switch roles.

LIFTOFF | 51

Pressing her feet against his chest will let him plunge in deep, completely filling her up. If he holds on to her hips, he'll have more control over his movements and can support her once she detonates from the sheer pleasure of it.

52 UP IN ARMS

Planting zigzag kisses along the soft area on the inside of his forearm is a swoon move for when she wants to slow, but not cool down, the fun and games.

COOK'S CHOICE | 53

Having a table to lean against means the angle of penetration can be easily adjusted for him to enter her from behind vaginally or anally, as his cravings take him.

54 EVERYTHING BUT . . .

While he's still clothed—belt buckled, pants zipped—she can give him a dressed blow job, placing her mouth over his groin and exhaling hotly while running her fingers up and down his legs and across his belly. He may get impatient and rip his own pants off!

SPIN THE TOP 55

She merry-go-rounds his pole, swinging her body to create momentum. Not an easy move to master, the happy news is that the only way to get good at it is with lots of full-body practice.

56 DIRTY KISSES

What lifts an orgasm from good to truly great is building up the blood flow to the pelvis. She can get him pumping double-time with a trail of smooches along his sensitive inner thighs.

CORE-GASM 57

Adding sit-ups to this pose can have the double effect of making it easier to hold for longer but also making it unnecessary, since the extra up-and-down movement can stimulate her vagus nerve and trigger a high-power orgasm.

58 LAZY-BOY

Don't be fooled by the name. This pose is anything but. Not only will he need to be flexible, limber, and able to leap tall buildings in a single bound—she'll need a six-pack to stay balanced and another for drinking once they collapse (in about three minutes).

FULL THROTTLE | 59

The combined stimulation of his tongue and a small vibrator means that multiple orgasms are just around the corner.

60 GIVING LIP

The best DIY orgasm assistant is a vibrator—but placing it directly on her clit can actually backfire and minimize sensation. Instead, the hot spot to aim for is the upper tip where the protective hood is.

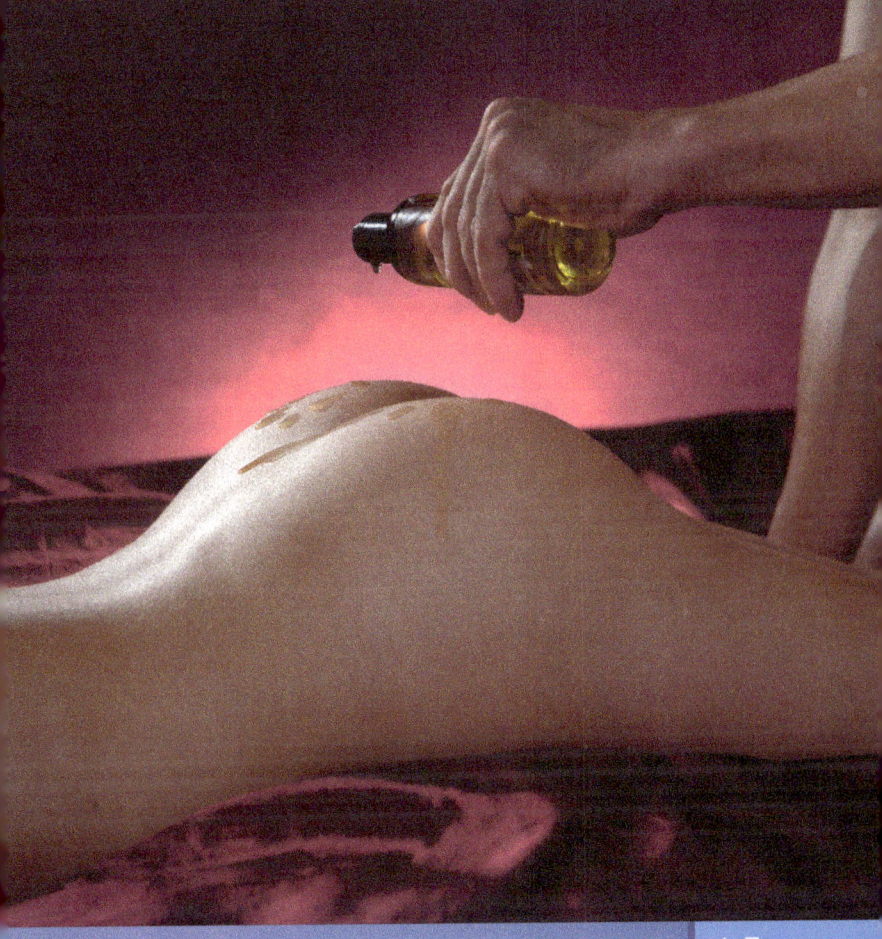

DROP BY DROP 61

A little goes a long way with massage oil, so he should drip it out slowly rather than pour it. To keep her simmering with anticipation, he can drizzle it in random patterns over her skin before rubbing it in.

62 IN HIS HEAD

Gently massaging his scalp relaxes him and gets him in the mood. To give her rubdown a raunchy edge, she can move her fingers in small circles, pressing down to stimulate the receptive nerve endings wall-to-wall on this part of the body.

THE PLOW | 63

This is an equal opportunity pose because although it requires men to sow deep, both partners must be fully engaged in the moment to reap the full benefits.

64 SPIRAL

He can use his tongue to trace tiny, tantalizing circles in the center of her palm, in a gradual, oh-so-slowly widening motion.

PEEP SHOW | 65

Allowing him to sit back and enjoy the show has the triple-X effect of turning him on, giving herself the kind of attention she craves, and showing him exactly what strokes she likes.

66 MINDLESS WORK

The vertical angle of this pose means she can play with depth and speed, going faster, slower, harder, deeper, up and down, round and round, giving his love muscle a tip-to-toe workout.

CHEEKY GIRL | 67

His cheek stubble isn't just Hollywood sexy—it's also dense with feel-good receptors that she can stimulate with a few well-executed scratches.

68 CROW'S NEST

Unless lovers are a similar height, they're going to need coordination, strength, and balance to make a vertical merger work. But lifting her leg and leaning back to arch her back slightly turns this into a pose anyone can do—and has the happy side effect of pressing his pelvic bone against her clitoris with every thrust.

BLIND DATE | 69

Taking away one sense can intensify the others, so blindfolding her and then teasing her with feathery flicks, strokes, and touches might be all it takes to give her a mind-searing, bed-rattling orgasm.

70 IN SYNC

He'll cry, "Ooooooh!" and go straight to pleasure heaven if she can fondle his head and rub his ear at the same time.

PLAT DU JOUR | 71

This on-the-table passion platter puts her derrière
at just the right height for him to feast his eyes—
and more, should the urge take him.

72 SECRET RAPTURE

His script: to pounce and press her down, breathing sweet nothings—or perhaps sexy somethings—in her ear.

LOVE BITES | 73

People have a slightly higher tolerance for pain when they're aroused, so he can power-thrust her sexed-up state to the next level by giving the thin skin on her inner thighs a little nibble before bestowing the full oral treatment.

74 BOTTOM'S UP

He can take oral sex to a steamier level by taking some time to explore her anal area while he's in the neighborhood.

GETTING CHEEKY | 75

Her face is actually one of the cream-of-the-crop hot spots, so he should use a light touch and vary the pressure by switching strokes between the knuckles of one finger, his fingertips, and the back of his hand.

76 TOP SECRET TOUCH

Taking a break from making out to lick, suck, and nibble the sweet fleshy spot of his earlobe will send electric currents all the way down to his package.

LIFT UP | 77

Here's a scintillatingly sly way to add more ooomph to this pose—instead of pushing her hips into his, she plays with the angle by moving up and down on her tippy-toes.

78 PLUMP IT UP

A quick squeeze to her nipples will make them swell slightly, priming them for more intense attention from his mouth.

WHO'S THE BOSS? | 79

He won't have to work overtime as he gets down to business—his hands can do double duty, guaranteeing an outcome that's not only speedy but also sensational.

80 | ALL TIED UP

He'll feel like her sex toy and beg for release when she restrains him with a pair of rubber (more comfortable than metal) cuffs and has her wicked way with his body. She can use her power to allow him to climax or withhold stimulation for a tortuous minute or two.

UP CLOSE AND PERSONAL | 81

A brush of the lips can have the same erotic
impact as intimate eye contact when bodies
are pressed à deux in a sweet embrace.

82 TOOLED FOR FUN

Using a Fleshlight is a huge step up for self-pleasuring because it lets him give his love muscle the supertight sensation he craves without his hand ending up stuck in a death grip.

TIGHT END | 83

A deep penetrating move that doesn't allow for a lot of in-and-out—but who needs it when there's loads of delicious pressure? He can help her keep the big squeeze on by pressing her legs together and gently moving them to and fro.

84 STOCKING FILLER

He won't wait for an invitation to lavish her body with kisses when she climbs into bed wearing sexy thigh-highs and nothing else.

SHOW YOUR TONGS | 85

A hot variation of the Kama Sutra classic, getting on top for a woman is all about feeling good about herself and creating some feel-good action. That means going ahead and grinding her pelvis into his, leaning back, and showing off her curves. He won't be able to keep his hands off her.

86 CLOSE SHAVE

It takes a brave woman to trust her man to go near her privates with a razor. To keep the action out of the emergency room, she should soften her skin by taking a warm shower before he starts and trim her tresses with nail scissors. A dab of hypoallergenic cream after will soothe things and get the sparks flying.

NAIL HIM | 87

The Kama Sutra describes three different ways to use nails during foreplay: pressing, marking, or scratching—but never to do any of them until the amorous action is cranked up high or the result will be the wrong kind of stimulation.

88 FOOT JOB

This move stands and delivers if he or she has a foot fetish. But it's worth stepping into even if they don't. In the ancient practice of reflexology, certain pressure points in the feet can set off a full-body meltdown when stimulated.

MIRROR, MIRROR ON THE WALL | 89

Holding a hand mirror between her legs while she takes care of business lets her fantasize about another girl being in on the fun or simply appreciate the amazing way her labia change color and the entire area gets wet as she loves herself.

90 ON THE BENCH

This elevated take on the wheelbarrow actually minimizes the amount of brute strength the move usually calls for, so both he and she can ride it out for as long as it takes.

PICTURE PERFECT | 91

Snapping naughty pictures together can be a very seductive form of foreplay, where one person plays the part of director and the other is the star of the shoot. She'll feel more comfortable striking a pose if he's also naked.

92 RIDE HIM HARD

Hard whacks are best kept to the butt when using a riding crop. She can mix pleasure and pain by alternating between little hits and light taps with the tip from toes to chest, skimming—but not quite touching—his package, teasing him into a frenzy until he begs for mercy.

DOGGY ON THE TABLE | 93

This pose is an exotic melting pot of sensual moves in that it opens her wide so he can penetrate her bottom deeply and thrust to his and her fullest potential. It's not very intimate—which means it's best tried by those experienced with anal sex.

94 BUTTER UP

A couple doesn't need to be into S&M to get slaphappy—he'll find that the lightest pat on her bottom can up her rapture factor, pumping up her adrenaline and making her heart race.

THE G-FORCE 95

A little lift of her bottom gives his rod true aim to hit the oh-ooh-oooh so sensitive G-spot on the front wall of her vajayjay. He'll be putting in most of the in-and-out effort, but she'll need to pay attention to keep in sync with him.

96 TRESS TEASE

To give her a jingle from head to toe while they're heave-hoeing, he can hold on and tug her locks as he comes in and release a little as he goes out.

OFFICE SPACE | 97

This cozy pose will work just as well in a small cubicle as it will in a corner office and is so easy to execute that couples will want to make it part of their daily tasks.

98 SHOTGUN

Who's in charge depends on how she angles herself—if she leans back against him, he's in the driver's seat as he bounces her up and down on his knees. If she leans forward, she can take the controls and give him a wild ride.

PAY LIP SERVICE 99

Instead of using full-force suction on her nipples, he can switch-hit between kissing them and brushing the tips with his lip and tongue. The rough-soft combo will make her points stand on end.

100 SADDLE UP

While the logistics of this move are not complicated, he'll need complete command of his sexual muscles because it's pretty much guaranteed to result in a full-body, off-the-Richter-scale climax for her (he'll benefit from her seismic aftershocks).

MOVING MOUNTAINS | 101

This pose requires a lot of upper-body strength from both him and her, but the passion payoff is that she stays in complete control of his pace while he gets a bird's-eye view of the terra firma.

102 SUNDAY HAMMOCK

She should plan on putting in all the erotic effort here, whirligigging around his groin by sitting tall, leaning forward and then back.

DEEP THROAT | 103

Gently stroking up and down along the length of his throat will soon make him putty in her hands.

104 SATISFACTION GUARANTEED

This position has it all—deep penetration, loads of fabulous friction, access to all her parts, and a front seat view of the action. If she's shy about taking her pleasure into her own hands, he can easily reach around and do the honors.

PEELING AND REVEALING 105

A really good blow job is a long, drawn-out, teasing affair. Gently pulling down his underwear until just the head of his shaft is peeking out will give her plenty of flesh to work mouth magic on before stripping him naked.

106 NAIL ART

Since his chest is especially sensitive, she'll have to be a little forceful when dragging her nails against the skin—but not so rough that she leaves welts.

SPEED BUMPS | 107

Because the angle of this pose acts like a Wonderbra on her breasts, she can give him a happy ride between the girls no matter what her cup size is.

108 | KISS-OFF

Once the nookie starts, most lovers keep their eye on what's going on down below. Slipping in a few smooches midcanoodle will intensify the connection, especially if they mimic sex play—hard and horny lipsmackers when the action is intense, and soft, romantic kisses when the love play starts slowing down.

MAN ON A MISSION | 109

This slow-build variation on missionary presses flesh against flesh, making it a go-to position when he and she feel the desire to be connected. To heighten the friction, she can add some swivel to her hips as he plunges in and out.

110 SITTING PRETTY

Because this close pose sends him in deep, she doesn't need to do much more to get sweaty than sway forward and back with a gentle rubbing motion.

HANDS-ON | 111

Too many men twist her nipples as if they were trying to tune them in. But all it takes to dial up some pleasure for these little knobs is a gentle pull or pinch.

112 TEASING STRIP

He can turn getting naked into a foreplay fest by slowly peeling off each piece of her clothing, one by one, taking the time to lick, stroke, nibble, and generally adore every inch of her bare flesh as it's gradually exposed.

ONCE BITTEN | 113

A little nip on the nip can be more intense than licking or sucking and is a deliciously quick way to amp up the action.

114 NAVEL-GAZING

The ultrathin skin running from just below the chest to just above the pelvis is one long, orgasmic runway, begging to be landed on with lots of loving kisses.

ON THE SIDE | 115

While a vibrator is a sure-fire salacious side dish to bring to the table, the kitchen is chockablock full of homemade passion props from a fridge stocked with ice, cream, and other erotic edibles to the kitchen sink water sprayer and drawers with of all sorts of naughty implements like spatulas and whisks.

116 DEEP IMPACT

If he's on the lookout for her G-spot, the chances are excellent that he's about to find it. For full impact, she can arch her back to suck him in even more.

KEEP HIM ON HIS TOES 117

A good blow job is a little unpredictable. She can alternate between sucking, stroking, squeezing, slurping, and swirling or even sliding a vibrator into the mix.

118 POSTERIOR PICKUP

Let the rumpus begin! The relatively denser muscle mass in this area means that he wants her to push his tush with loads of lip pressure.

MYSTERY LOVER | 119

Her from-behind approach can be a huge fantasy turn-on for him, as he closes his eyes and gets lost in a scorching daydream.

120 CLASSIC TWINING

An all-purpose move ideal for lovers whose below-the-belt regions are not a perfect match, she can keep things tight by opening her legs just enough to let him in. Then, once he's in place, she can clamp her legs to work up that tight, loving feeling.

KNEEL AND DELIVER 121

It's surprising what a difference a change of angle can make when it comes to sensation. Him kneeling during a blow job is the simplest of alterations, but it could blow his mind!

122 SNUGGLY

Curled up, body-to-body, her chest pressed against his back and her hands free to stray around up front makes this definitely not a PG-rated cuddle!

KEEP YOUR HANDS TO YOURSELF | 123

Turning masturbation from a solo to interactive affair can boost intimacy. Couples can make a game of it and try to finish in sync or even see who can get themselves to the finish line first. Winner takes all.

124 | PUPPY LOVE

This kneel-stand trick means he can throw her more than a bone during sex—his hands are free to go for a walk all over her breasts and clit.

SEAMLESS KISS | 125

The secret sizzle spots on the body are anywhere that it bends—the inner elbow, the wrist, the waist, the back of the knee. Grazing his way around these areas will make her beg for More! More! More!

126 LITTLE PIGGIES

The soles of the feet are an acupressure sweet spot. Pressing about one-third of the way down from the middle toe can cause energy to travel up the legs to the pelvis and make her feel hot to trot.

HIT THE TRIGGER | 127

The hands-on nature of a bullet vibrator means he controls exactly where and how it moves. Translation: He can give her what she wants, exactly when she needs it, and give himself a buzz at the same time.

128 TOOTSIE TREAT

Chances are her feet are aching from having been crammed into high heels all day. Using his thumb and forefinger to pull gently, twist, and then rub below her toes will work faster than a Dirty Martini to get her to kick back and chill.

STAND TALL | 129

She can custom-order her orgasm and flip
his switch at the same time by taking matters
into her own hand while making love.

130 RELAX AND RELEASE

The neck and shoulders carry a lot of stress. A racy rubdown can be just what the doctor ordered to romantically reconnect.

BENCH PRESS BLOW JOB | 131

She can give his favorite muscle a strenuous workout—and the best part is he's finished with his sets when he climaxes.

132 DESK DUTY

No one will be jockeying for a better position when trying this move at work. It requires very little effort and time but delivers on thrills—making it ideal for a quick lunchtime tryst.

CLEAN SWEEP | 133

No extreme makeover is required to turn the kitchen into a delectable den of love. But the room is lined with sharp items like knives and scissors, so lovers should make sure they give the area a clean sweep before getting carnal.

134 HEAD-ON

A gentle kiss on the forehead is like a sweet, wordless promise of love.

THE MIND-BENDER | 135

She'll need a few yoga lessons before mastering this move, but having her head pointed down and her back arched means she'll get the double whammy of an amazing mental blood rush and priming her pelvis in perfect G-spot poke position.

136 | COFFEE BREAK

Sitting on top and grinding circles around his member is not something she'll want to do nine-to-five. Resting her hands on the back of a chair will take some of the pressure off her legs without losing momentum.

SOIXANTE-NEUF | 137

Ah, the infamous classic. Definitely, every couple should dive into a 69 every now and then. But since most people aren't good enough at multitasking to both achieve and bestow orgasm at the same time, it shouldn't become a couple's go-to oral plat du jour.

138 SLICK STROKES

Simply smearing oil on her breasts and rubbing it in will make her feel like a chicken getting prepped for roasting. Much more sensual and romantic is for him to pour the oil into his hands first, rub them together to warm things up, and then gently cup them around each breast, massaging upward toward the nipples.

SHOWER YOUR SENSES | 139

Getting spic and span is beside the point. Getting steamed up prepares the body for a thrill by loosening muscles (great for flexibility) and increasing circulation, making the body more receptive to touch.

140 BACKING IT UP

Many women are shy about guiding him to their posterior, but depth isn't necessary to bring her to the brink of bliss—a few frisky fingertip fondles around the area will be enough to send her though the roof.

ENTWINED LOVERS 141

The pleasure in this tight pose is its restrictions. It sets both partners up for deeper penetration and allows him to slow his thrusts. Rather than move in and out, he can use gentle rocking motions to give constant, consistent, crazy-good stimulation to her G-spot.

142 MILK AND WATER EMBRACE

In this intense embrace, lovers connect spiritually and physically to become one—hearts are pressed together and arms clasp each other tight.

A WORD IN HIS EAR | 143

All it takes is a simple kiss accompanied by promises of what's to come whispered seductively in his ear to make even the strongest man whimper.

144 | 68 REDUX

For a naughty twist on the classic 69, couples pull a quick switch and work their fingers into the action instead. Warning: The results are guaranteed to burn a hole in the bedsheets.

NAUGHTY NURSE | 145

All it takes to make his temperature rise is a flirty nurse cap. But she'll really send his pulse rate into overtime if she offers to give him a sponge bath—with her tongue.

146 PET THE POOCH

The extra friction created by him giving her a bone from behind while patting her in the front is sure to make her sit up and beg.

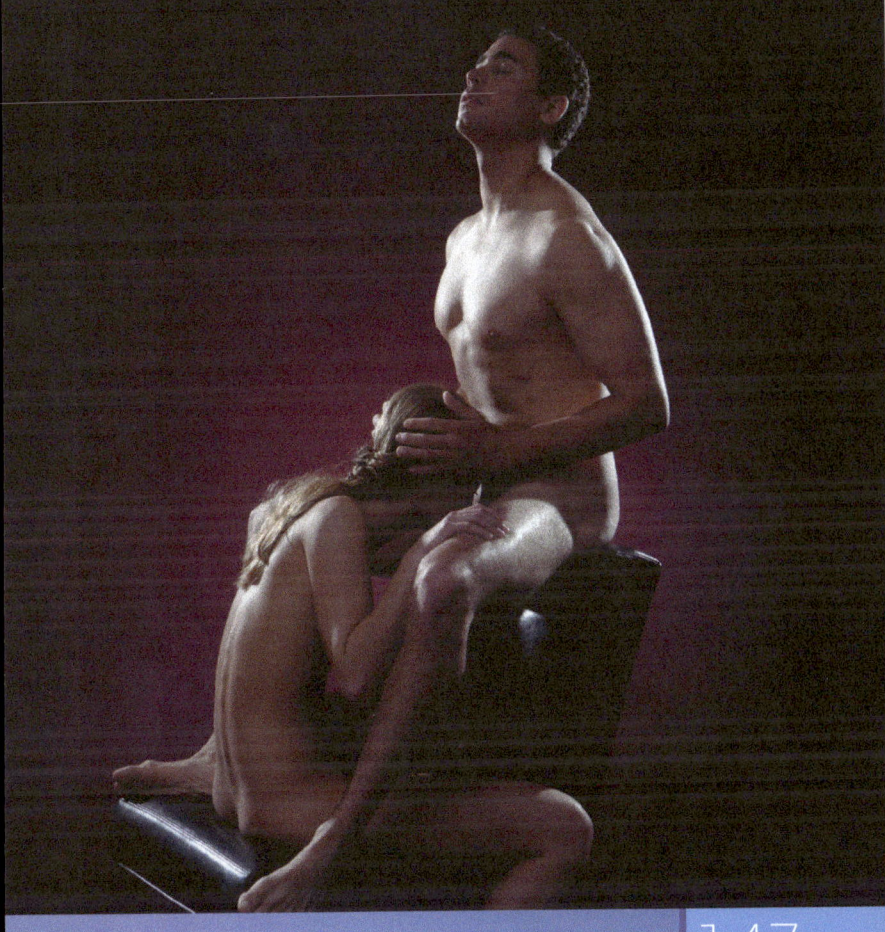

BLOW THE MAN DOWN | 147

The easy access to his tackle means she can blow his mind by mouthing off on him from every angle, especially often-missed places like the softer underside of his shaft and the sensitive patch of flesh between his sack and rod.

148 IGNITION SWITCH

It's easy for him to lose control in the moment and start caressing her breasts as if he were kneading bread dough. But because she's likely to be even more responsive to his touch right now, a little light pressure with his palms while gently squeezing her nipples between his fingers will do the trick.

RISE TO CRESCENDO | 149

Varied stimulation is the key for her to leap from one orgasm to another. To help her hit the peak again . . . and again . . . and again, he can simply change the area of her body that he's caressing once she climaxes.

150 AB-SOLUTELY AHHH!

His entire chest is an erogenous zone, but there's one particular destination that'll spark more goose bumps than any other part—the area just above his belly. The skin is thinner there, and there's not as much fatty tissue underneath (especially if he's sporting a six-pack), so licking here is going to feel pretty darned good.

FRYING HIS CORNDOG | 151

Adding a chair and table to the original cowgirl pose means the ride will be twice as wild and ten times as good, as she rotates her hips and rises up and down to tease his wrangler until it's frothing.

152 LOVER'S PORN

Couples can grab a copy of erotic lit and take turns reading the steamier passages to each other . . . taking time out to reenact some of them. Seductively whispering, using a throaty purr, or playing around with different accents will keep the action bawdy instead of blushing.

CORE POWER | 153

She can load the weight on or keep things light by adjusting how much she leans forward and backward on him.

154 | 68

It may be one short of 69, but this pose may pack an even more powerful pleasure punch because the type of stimulation is varied, making it easier for lovers to duck and dive at the same time.

TAKE A POSITION | 155

Her job, should she choose to accept it, is to lie back and wantonly let him ravish her. Orgasms will be included in the benefits package.

156 TAILGATING

He can use his mouth anywhere he touches her with his hands—the warm wetness will feel more intense than even the softest caress.

TENDER TOUCH | 157

An erotic bottom massage can be an especially affectionate way to after-play and keep the intimate connection postclimax—and possibly a prelude to even more hot and heady sexual magic!

158 ROSEBUD

She can book a Brazilian wax and then wrap it up in a sexy G-string as a saucy bombshell gift for him to discover as he undresses her.

LIE BACK AND ENJOY | 159

Here's a pose that's restful but also opens her up completely for him: The entire front of her body is exposed, and he can reach around and trail behind as she drags the vibrator from her breasts to her clitoris without interrupting the oral fun

160 ON HIS KNEES

It requires a bit more finesse (read: effort), but the view she gets of him going to work makes it worth it! If she has good balance, she can use her leg to lock and load his head into position when he hits one of her high notes.

TIPPING POINT | 161

The outer third of the vajayjay is a thin-skinned nerve terminal, making it an ideal place for his shaft to maintain a happy holding position when he wants to slow things down until she catches up.

162 MAKE YOUR MARK

Bling is not a girls-only option. A pair of nipple clamps will turn a blow job into a whoa job.

KNEES UP | 163

Hands freely roam in this position. Because the easy access to her body means he'll be hitting all her right spots, she'll need to hold on to him for balance. He can then caress her breasts and torso before sliding down for some between-the-legs love play.

164 RUB A DUB DUB

The key difference between an oh-your-poor-throbbing-feet massage and an ooh-la-la erotic foot rub is the pressure used—to give things a titillating tingle, lovers should skip the soft strokes and squeeze hard on the big toe and the sides and heel of each foot.

KISS YOUR MISS | 165

Who says a kiss is just a kiss? Passionate smooches before and during sex intensify love play by cranking up blood pressure and causing the heart to beat faster—which makes it easier to get in the mood and reach orgasm.

166 | THE CAPPUCCINO

Skip the morning caramel latte! Sex on a kitchen table is fast, frothy, and fabulous—especially when he stirs her legs to create even more friction. The secret recipe? He should penetrate her before she lifts her legs.

SLOW STRIP | 167

The key to keeping the sexual tension high while disrobing is always to stay in physical contact with each other, kissing and caressing while removing clothing piece by tantalizing piece.

168 STARFISH

The mind-blowing maneuver in this saucy twist on woman-on-top is for her to rock back and side to side instead of up and down. To make things more intense, she can push her legs together, practically guaranteeing endless pleasure and pressure on her clit.

ALL CHOKED UP | 169

Lightly placing hands around the neck during sex will reduce circulation to the brain and intensify orgasm. To keep things safe, she should wait until he is actually climaxing before applying pressure—and stop when he tells her to.

170 THE NAUTILUS

Most men zero in on a woman's nipples, but the Kama Sutra recommends moving around them in ever-narrowing circles to draw her sexual energy toward her buds.

IN THE DEEP | 171

Putting her legs on his chest is a variation on the usual woman-on-top leg straddle. But she should go slow—some women find that the resulting ultradeep penetration can be a little uncomfortable if her lover is larger than average.

172 MAGIC TOUCH

To really boost the mercury, she can add some verbal blow-by-blows as she shows him exactly how she pleases herself. He may not be able to wait until she finishes before jumping in on the action.

KISSING THE YONI 173

Yoni is the Sanskrit word for vagina but is also, loosely translated, the sacred space. He can pay tribute to hers with The Quivering Kiss: He lightly pinches the tip of her labia and kisses them as though he were nuzzling the lower lip of her mouth.

174 THE PUSH

Pleasure will be her mission when she uses her hands to lightly press her legs down, causing her pelvis to grind deliciously against his.

HOT HANDS | 175

A sure-fire way for him to heat her up—even when she says she isn't in the mood—is with a full-body massage. But when time is tight, a little TLC (tender loving caresses) to her pins will quickly pep up her passion.

176 FINGER-LICKING GOOD

Any part of the body can be a stand-in for the genitals. So while making out and touching each other, lovers should take time to suck on bits like the fingers to give a taste of the mouth moves planned for below the belt.

OLYMPIC ORGASMS | 177

The tongue is the body's strongest muscle, but for her to feel the burn, he'll need to use consistent, steady strokes that move across as well as up and down her clit.

178 LIGHT DUTIES

When she's on top, her weight can sometimes put too much pressure on his power tool. Using the desk chair helps her ease up and move around in new motions or adjust her position now and then without draining him.

LAP DANCE | 179

Apart from controlling the depth and intensity, this position lets her rock to her own beat and mix up the playlist by either bouncing, gyrating backward and forward, or swaying side to side.

180 TORRID TUTORIAL

Pretending to be a naughty coed who needs to be taught a (sexy) lesson is a fun way for a couple to introduce some steamy spanking to their passion play.

ON THE WATERFRONT 181

Remove slippery objects before attempting this three-footed pose. He'll find it easier to gain access if he bends at the knees. If he holds on tight, she can lean back so that the water cascades over their bodies.

182 | GAME NIGHT

Some fast, no-frills, spontaneous fun can deliver instant gratification to lovemaking along with a hot dollop of triple-X seasoning.

CLIMBING THE TREE | 183

Lovers will have to be almost the same height to get into this position. But once they find their center of balance, they'll be able to exchange all manner of scorching strokes, caresses, pinches, and kisses while gazing into each other's eyes.

184 STRADDLE CUDDLE

This cozy switch on woman-on-top turns what's usually a high-energy move into a tender moment by connecting lovers heartbeat to heartbeat.

JUMP START | 185

He can pinch her nipples when stimulating her breasts, but not the way he did to tease his little brother. She prefers a gentle squeeze, followed by caresses to the entire breast.

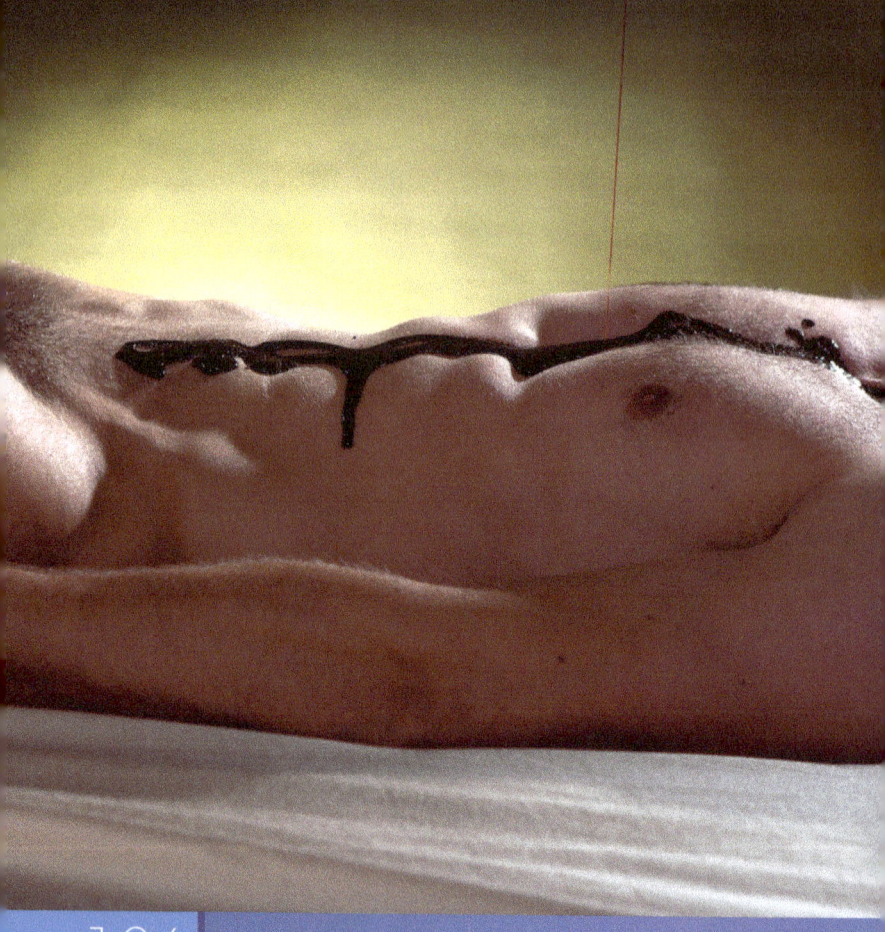

186 SEXY TOPPING

Dribbling chocolate sauce on his belly and slowly licking it off will satisfy more than her sweet tooth. Bonus: Chocolate contains the chemical phenylethylamine (PEA), which can turn an orgasm into an especially rich and tasty treat.

THE LIONESS | 187

When done with just the right pressure, a nail dragging across the skin can send shivers up his spine and prep him for a wild night of jungle love.

188 LAZY-GIRL

She can play with the type of stimulation he gives her and keep him jazzed by alternating between arching her back for an up-down stroke and lifting her hips for an in-out rub a dub.

OFFICE ORAL | 189

A little "afternoon delight" in the work station can perk up those long postlunch hours. Those who have been skipping after-hours visits to the gym can get the same tasty results without the muscle burn if she perches on the edge of the desk.

190 DOUBLE WHAMMY

On-the-side poses like these usually mean limited movement, but the sneaky bonus is that his hand can slide around to be in easy reach of her sweet spot. But he should be prepared—the heady combination of getting a rubdown while having him deep inside her may cause her to twist and shout.

SACRED SACRUM | 191

The hollow of her back (just above her bottom) contains sacral nerves that shoot straight to her genitals and can even trigger a mind-melting orgasm when gently pressed with the palm of the hand.

192 SECRET RUSH

Soft breathy licks, kisses, nibbles, and sucks on unexpected and ultrasensitive areas—such as the back of the knees or the inside of the ankles—may be make her giddy with lust . . . or may dissolve her into giggly laughter because the sensation ends up feeling more ticklish than tantalizing.

ALL BASES COVERED | 193

All her systems are go-go-go when he extends foreplay into the actual game plan, continuing to kiss and caress her in a triple-base move while making love.

194 LOOK, DO TOUCH

A silky sexy bra-and-underwear combo makes her look sexy without even trying and is sure to warm him up without her laying so much as a finger on him.

SHEER DELIGHT | 195

For extra urgency, she should keep her G-string on so that he can pull it to one side and penetrate her with his tongue.

196 GALLOPING HORSE

This on-top-of-it pose means that not only will she be able to control how fast, furious, and far he rides into her, she can also mix up her pleasure trip by moving backward and forward and side to side.

U GO, GIRL! | 197

Easily missed during lovemaking, her U-spot, the small area of tissue above the urethra and right below the clit, can be caressed for a simple yet superb way to get satisfaction when she's taking her pleasure into her own hands.

198 GIVE HIM A HAND

While the mouth is where the action is, she can use her hands on the side. If she's talented at multitasking, alternating spanks between slow and soft and fast and hard will hyperspeed him into sensory overload.

CUDDLE UP | 199

The intense connective energy in this pose is all about soulful, sweet eye-gazing that lets couples snuggle and have sex.

200 PRASARITA

This is a good stretching position if a previously vigorous romp left her stiff, tired, and tense. The deep bend not only loosens her muscles but also widens her so he can slip right in.

UNDER PRESSURE | 201

The amount of nerve endings in the inner thigh makes this area ultrasensitive. Pinches should be on the gentle side, as anything more than a light tweak will make her cry "Owww!" instead of Ohhh!"

202 MAGIC MIRROR

Watching her masturbate with a mirror gives him an up close and personal peek at what makes her pant. He'll love it—as long as she promises him that he can have his turn.

LAP IT UP | 203

Everyone can use a little tease before they please. Here, she lowers down on to his lap but stops well short of penetration to delicately slide her petals back and forth over his shaft. Only once everyone is whetted and wetted may the full fun commence.

204 | ON THE MOUND

The purpose of a yoni massage is not sexual pleasure—though that might be a happy side effect. Instead, the idea is to create an emotional-spiritual-sensual connection that naturally awakens sexual energy. Ommmmm.

EASY RIDER | 205

She gets to control the pace and depth of this joy ride, but he gets to direct the action with his hips and hands. Once this trot takes off, he can push her forward on to all fours and gallop to climax from behind.

206 IN HIS FACE

A few sweet, light kisses on his chin, jaw line, cheeks, forehead, even his nose will inspire all sorts of warm, fuzzy feelings. But she should avoid wet, sloppy licks, or the only response she'll prompt is an image of his dog.

COWPOKE | 207

Reverse cowgirl is bottoms-up the best choice for beginners to anal sex. It lets her control the speed, depth, and angle of penetration while his hands can roam her range and keep her bucking like a bronco.

208 ORAL BUZZ

When she holds the toy down near his lips as he licks her, his mouth will experience an arousing tingly ting ting while transmitting the vibes to her.

CHILD'S POSE | 209

This ultrarestful position is ideal for trying anal sex for the first time, as it keeps her body completely relaxed while opening her nether regions to penetration.

210 | WAKE-UP CALL

Taking a sip of hot coffee or tea before taking him in her mouth will give him an eye-opening oral treat. To avoid scalding him, she should hold the warm liquid in her mouth for a few seconds to heat things up and then swallow before swallowing him.

FLYING HIGH | 211

Something as simple as raising her up on a table or desk can transform any rear entry or anal pose into a crash and burn, baby, burn moment.

212 HANDY ON THE JOB

This is hands-down the best pose for her to stroke him into submission. It allows her to sit comfortably while she works her digital magic, and to see the results without fear of him collapsing on her once she's detonated him.

RISING POSITION 213

Although this move encourages loads of deep, delicious thrusting, it's not easy for her to hold very long, so he may want to slide down to his knees if it looks like she's on the verge of collapse.

214 DRESS FOR SEX-CESS

When she slips into some bold underthings, he's going to know exactly what's on her mind—something sexy!

CROSSOVER 215

A high-octane alternative to the usual constant thrusting is for both lovers to cross their legs. The extracurricular movement is for him to press her knees together, tightening her vajayjay around his shaft—which is never a bad thing!

216 LADY'S SQUEEZE

Arching her back and pressing her legs together will give him full access to the length of her vajayjay and the curve of her breasts. She can keep the action heart-pumping hot by rocking her pelvis and squeezing every time he enters her, then relaxing on the way out, then squeezing, then relaxing, then aaahhhhhh.

CORNER OFFICE 217

She won't mind being chained to the desk all day if this is the job description. He'll enjoy the view she presents as she lies back on the desktop like an open folder. This one also works well on the copier machine (collect all evidence after).

218 | SEXY SPOON

While it lacks the urgency or the deep penetration of other positions, it more than makes up for that in putting clitoral contact within Cool Hand Lover's reach.

COOKED TO ORDER | 219

Resting his head means he can feast long into the night because he's relieved of the usual neck strain that comes with an oral buffet.

220 GET WET

This is why detachable shower hoses were really invented! But it helps to grease up with some waterproof lube when having sex in the shower because the water washes away the body's natural juices, making thrusting more abrasive.

SPEAKING GREEK | 221

The ancient Greeks—who knew a thing or two about feel-good zones—ID'd the philtrum, the central ridge of the upper lip, as the sizzliest spot on the human body. Lightly tug, and she'll send a flare straight between his legs.

222 THE ARCH

Unlike full bridge, this half drawbridge doesn't require a lot of balance, but he'll still need to give her a lift up so she doesn't come crashing down as he thrusts in and out.

PULL THE PONY | 223

A light tug on her tresses will make her feel like she's being ravished, especially when pulled from behind. The key is for him to make his move during sex when her entire body is already amped for passion and to get close to the scalp so her neck doesn't feel like it's being yanked.

224 IN THE HOT SEAT

There are those who look at a chair and see only a common piece of household furniture. But the sexually adventurous will recognize it as a versatile sex prop for all sorts of passionate play—none of which involves just sitting around.

DRESSING DOWN | 225

Her usual go-to outfit at the end of a long workday is probably sweats, but a matching silk set is just as comfy and much less of a mood killer.

226 AB-SOLUTELY FABULOUS

By lightly pushing on her lower tummy just above the pelvic bone during nookie, he'll zero in on her G-spot, giving her an orgasmic shakedown that she'll feel from head to toe.

LYING WHEELBARROW 227

He amps up the lust leverage when he leans forward, power-boosting his thrust so he hits all her hot spots.

228 GOOD LIFT

Both partners will quickly realize why this crouching squat has gold-medal orgasm potential—hands are free to pinch-hit additional hot spots, while the slant is a perfect chance for her to work her PC muscles to stimulate his love muscle and for him to sink in deep and clean-jerk her G-spot.

BLUE PLATE SPECIAL | 229

He'll be doing most of the heavy lifting in this high-friction pose. Warning: He'll need to hold on tight to her hips, or his thrusting may send her sliding right off the table.

230 BUFF IT UP

A little prep will keep the sizzle passionate rather than painful when playing with wax. Use only pure paraffin wax candles during hot wax play, since they have the lowest temperature when they burn. Baby oil on the skin helps wax peel off easier, too. Start dripping from higher up so that the wax has more time to cool as it falls.

HOKEYPOKEY | 231

There's nothing soft or slow about this pose. She'll like the intense penetration, but what will really give the action its randy rhythm is if she shakes it all about against his groin as he moves in and out.

232 NEW NECKING

As he licks her neck, he can softly blow warm air over the wet patch. The combination of heat, moistness, and touch will give her shivers.

MOUNTING OF THE ASS | 233

A perfect pose for those spontaneous gotta-have-it-now moments, he might want to hold her waist in a tight caress so she doesn't fall flat on her face.

234 LADIES AND GENTS

Guys thrive on the show-stopping sensations a vibrator can bring to love play. So she shouldn't hesitate to introduce his work wand to hers during sex.

YEE-HAW! 235

Enough about pleasing him. This move is all about creating a carnal calamity and lassoing some lusty action for herself as she gyrates back and forth, side to side, and up and down, riding flat-backed on his stallion.

236 LOVER'S GAZE

Kissing his eyelids is an instinctual biological signal to him that she's totally in control of the love play, so he should lie back and take it like a man.

TOP AND TAIL | 237

She's on top—so she gets to direct where his tongue wanders. But this also means that he gets easy access to her backside and can cop a feel or ride a rim as the mood takes him.

238 DOUBLING DOWN

Her good parts are within lip-smacking reach when she's on top. For the ultimate high, he should keep it up as she explodes—which she definitely will, with double the pleasure.

NAKED SPOONING | 239

Like spooning only better, because they can custom-order their woo-hoo: anal sex, G-spot penetration, clitoral stimulation, breast caresses, testicle fondling, and perineum presses are all up for grabs. Best of all, she can fall asleep in his arms without moving an inch once the pleasure party is over.

240 TWISTED T

This pose is a little tricky, but it lets him come at her from all sides while keeping his hands free to explore her curves. Wait, it gets better. Because she can't move much, she can return the favor by concentrating on squeezing her pelvic or anal muscles to give him a no-hands rubdown.

TONGUE TICKLES | 241

He can give her a taste of what's to come by gently brushing her inner thighs with his lips and gradually following up with more passionate nuzzles until she's begging him to take the final plunge.

242 A LIGHT TOUCH

The clit is jam-packed with over eight thousand nerve endings. So caress it with an ultragentle, fast touch using just one or two fingers to get the sweetest results.

ANYWHERE BJ | 243

This all-purpose oral move means she can take the position and service him just about anywhere—making it ideal for stirring him up in the kitchen. Or at work. Or in the bedroom. Or the driveway. (Though she may need knee pads for the last one.)

244 TAINTED LOVE

It's important to have at least one sure-fire take-me-now inducing move—rubbing, tickling, and pressing the flesh between the anus and his or her sex organs is an easy one to master.

SHAKE AND BAKE | 245

When the craving is for a long, drawn-out session, she can slow the action down without lowering the temperature by withdrawing so that the tip of his shaft is resting against her clit. Shaking her hips so the head nestles against her moan zone adds just the right amount of spice.

246 GIVING POINTERS

Sucking on her fingers is a sensuously sly way for him to show her exactly what he'd like her to do to him when she's returning the favor on his—er—larger digit.

HAPPY BUDDHA 247

She can cop a trick from yoga to intensify the connection and grab her toes as he enters her. All on its own, this position completely opens her up to intense stimulation, but stretching her legs and pressing her hips against the floor will encourage him to go in even deeper.

248   EXTREME INTIMATE MAKEOVER

Sometimes, all that's needed is a new look to get the blood flowing in his loins. This not-your-grandma's underwear set is sexy without being skanky.

JUNGLE FEVER | 249

The erotic sensation of a strip of fur dragged and rubbed across the skin will soon have her blissfully swooning in his arms. Play with materials—mink, sable, and chinchilla are silky soft and the ultimate in luxury, while fox, rabbit, and coyote have a more textured feel, and rabbit gives a velveteen finish.

250 | WOMAN'S BEST FRIEND

She'll love the depth he can get in this position. Some men can go in so deep that the tip of the shaft nudges her cervix, an often-missed sweet spot.

HOLD 'EM | 251

All that's needed for a sexy card game is a deck of cards and changing the stakes of any standard game—Rummy, Poker, Crazy Eights, Hearts—to give it erotic rules, favors, and penalties. The best part? Losing!

252 LUNAR LAUNCH

He'll get a full-moon view of her posterior—which leads to all sorts of piquant possibilities: anal sex, classic rear entry, or even a little raunchy rump spanking.

DAILY GRIND 253

She might want to keep the heels on for this one—as long as her feet touch the ground, she can move her hips up and down and take full measure of his ruler.

254 BACKSTROKE

The back is surprisingly one of the hottest love triggers on the body—it's sensitive and oh-so divine, especially when lavished with loads of kisses.

SLIDE, BABY, SLIDE | 255

Instead of removing underwear before getting down and dirty, he can simply slide her panties to the side and have his wicked way with her.

256 | HERE, DOGGY!

She might want to get ready to howl with pleasure as he takes his fingers out for a walk in this classic woof position.

INTENSIFIED PLAY | 257

A woman needs a fair amount of muscle tension to reach orgasm. Crossing her arms behind her head and her ankles while he touches her is a no-sweat way to flex her body and heighten her sensitivity to sexual stimulation.

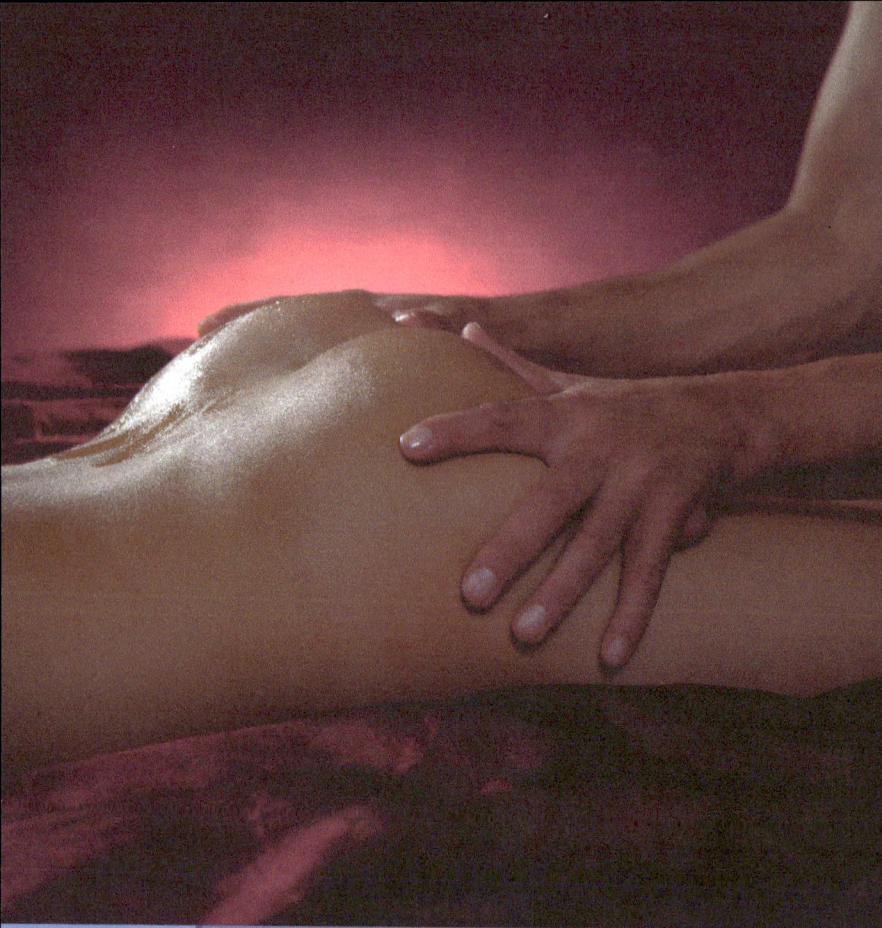

258 LET IT SLIDE

Massage oil adds a different kind of friction to foreplay, letting hands glide over every sweet spot on the body.

AFTERNOON DELIGHT | 259

This position is that rarest of things—extremely undemanding and very satisfying. The happy side effect is that this leaves plenty of opportunity for caresses and kisses.

260 TENDER MOMENTS

Taking time out to lovingly kiss her wrist is enough to make her swoon. But the area is also covered with an extremely fine layer of skin, which means that even the lightest lick will send a frisson of delight through her.

COZY CLASP 261

It can be difficult for her to move up and down when cuddled this tight, so for a can't-miss orgasm, she should lean forward and arch her back, keeping her groin nestled close to his.

262 | BREAST IS BEST

Even women who say having their nipples sucked makes them feel like a cow love it when he cups her breasts from underneath and lightly caresses her areola as he gently licks her nipples.

BACKWARD BEAR | 263

This reverse cuddle bonds lovers blissfully as it lets them touch head to toe without her feeling crushed—which can be the case in the man-on-top version.

264 KITCHEN ENCOUNTER

Grasping forearms means all of the action will be in the upper body as he pulls her up and she drags him back down. But the deep heat that comes from the chafing that the constant thrusting causes down below will be supersatisfying.

BODY PRESS 265

By holding her arms taut and pressing against her back with his tool, he'll make her feel completely exposed in front and covered from the rear, giving her total body titillation.

266 PLAYING HOT AND COLD

Licking a patch of her skin and then blowing hot air softly on the wet spot will pack a one-two wallop to her finish.

GRINDSTONE 267

In the right position, his body can be one huge self-pleasuring sex toy for her—by straddling one leg, she can rub herself against his thigh while his lips roam her breasts.

268 THE WRAP-UP

This is a slow, smooth, and sensual move, perfect for when fatigue sets in and no one is feeling all that creative or trying for seconds. Even if nothing momentous happens, the body-on-body closeness makes for some extraspecial after-canoodling coziness.

HEADREST 269

It's surprising the difference even a slight change in the angle of his dangle can make—for her as well as him. Lying on top of him puts her in total control of the action, which means she can expand her moves and give some TLC to his entire love triangle.

270 THIGH SIGH

Drawing his tongue along the length of her inner thigh will tease her ilioinguinal, a pleasure path that leads straight to her pelvis. Once she starts vibrating (and she most certainly will), he should give her the spot-on stroking she's craving.

BUNNY HOP | 271

He won't have to do much besides apply the lube (and perhaps scrape her off the ceiling with a spatula) when she brings a Rabbit to bed. To make her bunny hop, she should hold off turning it on until the ears are in place against the clit.

272 TAKE CHARGE

He loves it when she takes charge and treats him like her sexual plaything, making it clear that he's only there to pleasure her.

THE SKYPE IS THE LIMIT | 273

To go all the way with Skype and keep things lusty, it helps to go ultraslow and exaggerate every body movement to work in sync with the feed.

274 HUMPTY BUMPTY

They may do it in the movies all the time, but real-life couples should make sure the table can handle both their body weights along with the strain of the activities planned before hopping onboard.

TASTY TOE | 275

While there are hundreds of ways to nibble on each other, the Kama Sutra says that a gentle love bite on the big toe is sure to inspire urgent yearnings.

276 EASY GRAB

The only thing that she needs to do in this pose is arch back and whimper as he hits all her hot zones at once.

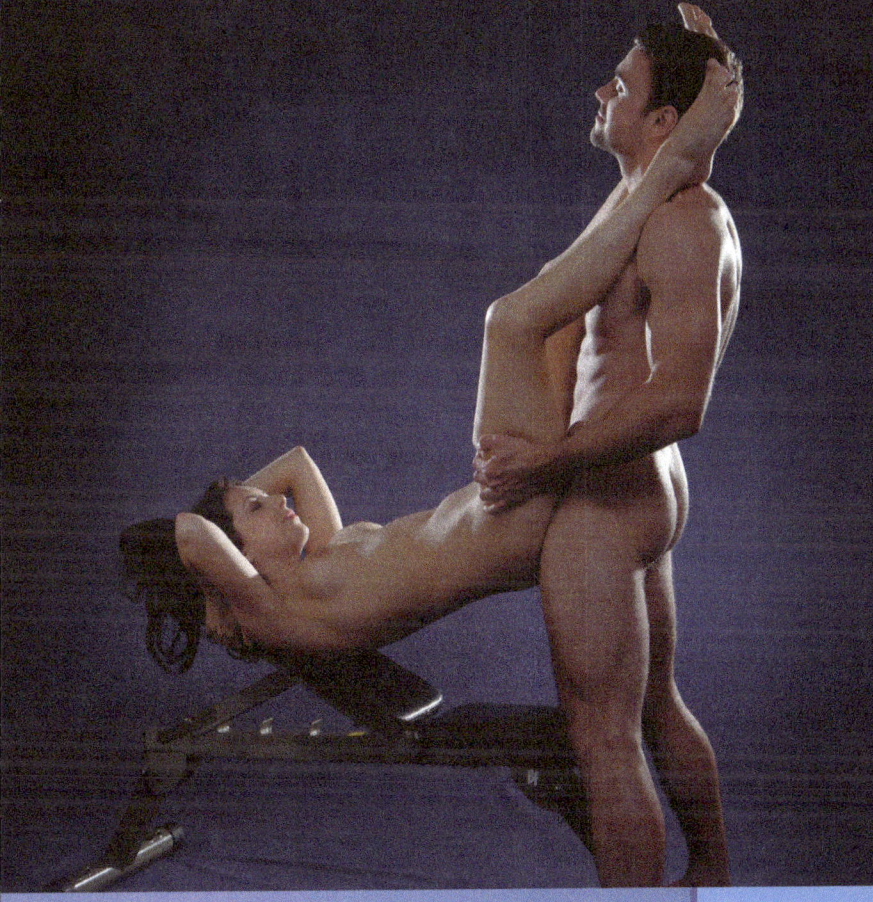

POSE WITH A VIEW | 277

This is a high-jinks pose that leaves her completely exposed to his lusty view. But she won't mind, since the aerobic angle also makes her stomach as flat as a washboard and her breasts perkier than a coffee machine.

278 BITE ME

His nipples cry out for a slightly rougher touch, making them a sweet spot for her to carefully sink her teeth into (leaving marks is not desirable).

FUR-TASTIC 279

Like a furry horsetail, this downy whip will give him a pleasant, soft sting on contact—more like a massage with impact than an actual blow. She can tease and torment him by tweaking her touch between flogs and furry tickles with the tips of the toy.

280 SUPPORTED BRIDGE

She shouldn't stay in this pose too long or she may pass out. But the volatile combination of the blood rush to her head and the maximum pressure his hand is putting on her clitoral area is going to make her collapse quickly anyway.

SEATED WHEELBARROW | 281

In this much more relaxed take on the traditional wheelbarrow, he's still in control, but it's easier to stay the course and hit the moan mark.

282 THE GENIE

Really focusing on one part of his body can be even more blissful than a head-to-toe rubdown. The secret is to use long, gliding strokes, putting more pressure pushing up and less going down. She'll know she's applying just the right amount of force because his spine won't be the only thing standing straight, at attention.

STEAM UP 283

There are no best sex positions in the shower.
It depends on flexibility and the space in the
bathroom. But this pose comes close to being
the most salacious, sensual, and simple.

284 BONKARAMA SPECIAL

A simple reverse cowgirl allows lovers to easily add a bit of what she fancies into the mix. It may not have a million different turning, bouncing bling bits, but a vibrator gets the job done. He can slip in from behind while she works her front end, and wowza!

AURAL LOVE | 285

Gently tugging and pinching the soft, fleshy part of her earlobes is a reliable method for creating waves of tingly pleasure throughout her body.

286 | SPECIAL TONIGHT

He won't be able to ignore her girls during the main event—or want to—when they're practically staring him in the face. Which is a good thing, since a little extra stimulation in this area during sex can supersize her orgasm in seconds.

BIG TOE | 287

There's a reason for the phrase "making your toes curl." A direct neurological link exists between the privates and the little piggies—especially the biggie. It turns out this reflex can be worked in reverse so that stimulating the big toe during sex can actually trigger an orgasm for her.

288 THE LOTUS

More like an intimate embrace than a sex position, the lotus doesn't leave much room for movement. Instead, both partners have to synchronize their body motion together by rocking instead of thrusting.

VIRTUAL FUN | 289

She should be prepared—the Fleshlight is so realistic that he may not know the difference between it and her when blindfolded. But that's half the fun! The other half is turning him on with her second "vagina."

290 PULL IT OFF

When she's in the mood for lovemaking, she can let him know it by grabbing him by the collar and slowly undressing him, giving him sexy smooches between each button. To really make him burn, she can slip his shirt on over her naked torso before completely ravishing him.

NIP TIPS | 291

With nipple clamps, breast play can be front and center during intercourse. Less is more when putting them on—the less skin pinched, the more it will be felt. Fifteen minutes is more than enough time to get a reaction—the really exquisite ache starts when the pressure is released.

292 MOUNTING ON THE BALL

No one will feel out of shape after mastering this deep-penetration pose. Balls that have sand in them help keep the action from rolling away.

ON TOP IS TOPS | 293

There's a reason woman-on-top rules as her all-time fave posish. She gets to take the libidinous lead and adjust her legs high for some joyful G-spot gyrations or low to bring him in deep, deep, deep—or high and low to hit all of her to-sigh-for spots at once.

294 SEED WITH RICE

Entwining bodies like this might not scorch sheets, but it creates a cozy connection that's ideal for intense intimacy and a sweet way to fall asleep after more rigorous romping.

WOMAN ON A MISSION | 295

Reach the Masters when he adds a set of nines to the play—he starts with nine shallow strokes, inserting only the head of his shaft before going for one full stroke. Next, he dips eight shallow strokes followed by two deep thrusts and so on until he's putting one shallow and nine full strokes. Fore!

296 JOYSTICK

She can easily make him break into a hot-and-heavy sweat with a few on-target squeezes along his love muscle. But to truly up the amorous ante, she should encircle his shaft with the forefinger and thumb of each hand and gently pull in opposite directions.

OPEN FOR BUSINESS | 297

A tricky pose that requires a very stable chair and strong hips, the turn-on return is deep penetration (for her) with a vivid view (for him)

298 THE YAWNING

Designed to do everything but make couples yawn, she opens herself entirely to him, pumping her PC muscles just enough to keep him at the edge of excitement.

LUSTY LIVELIHOOD | 299

The desk + chair combination offers lots of possibilities for fun. What makes it work is the varying heights of the furniture, which means that couples can experiment with a raunchy range of different poses without putting in a full day's work.

300 | G-SPOT FEAST

This is a difficult pose to hold for long, so she'll want things to cook up fast. Luckily, she can control the action by leaning forward for extra helpings of G-spot stimulation.

FEATHER FOREPLAY 301

Flicking a feather over a lover's most sensitive parts can feel like torture if they're very ticklish—and that's a good thing. Tickle therapy has been proved to reduce tension, making it exactly what the love doctor ordered after a high-stress day.

302 BLOW-BY-BLOW

She can take a break from blowing him by gently blowing on him—it'll slow down the action without bringing it to a complete stop.

SWITCH-HIT | 303

Taking time out during sex for a back-rub break may delay his climax, but will probably accelerate hers—especially if he uses a firm thumb press along her lower back that mimics the force his other appendage was applying lower down.

304 | CHILL OUT

A leg up from playing footsie, the proximity of the thighs to the naughty bits means this can be a relaxing way to cool down after a particularly heated romp or a raunchy way to get things sizzling again.

PLAYING ROUGH | 305

His nipples do not work like hers. He wants her to get rough with him and womanhandle his nips with little pinches, squeezes, kneads, and nail scratches.

306 TUG-OF-WAR

All the hip action actually comes from the arms—he pulls, she pulls. Everybody wins. (Her raised feet give her a bit more leverage, which she'll need to counterbalance his strength and prevent him from yanking her arms out of their sockets.)

TOPPING THE TABLE | 307

Not for the faint of heart—or, for that matter, weak of limb—this pose gets the blood pumping and, if she can hold it, delivers with an explosive orgasm.

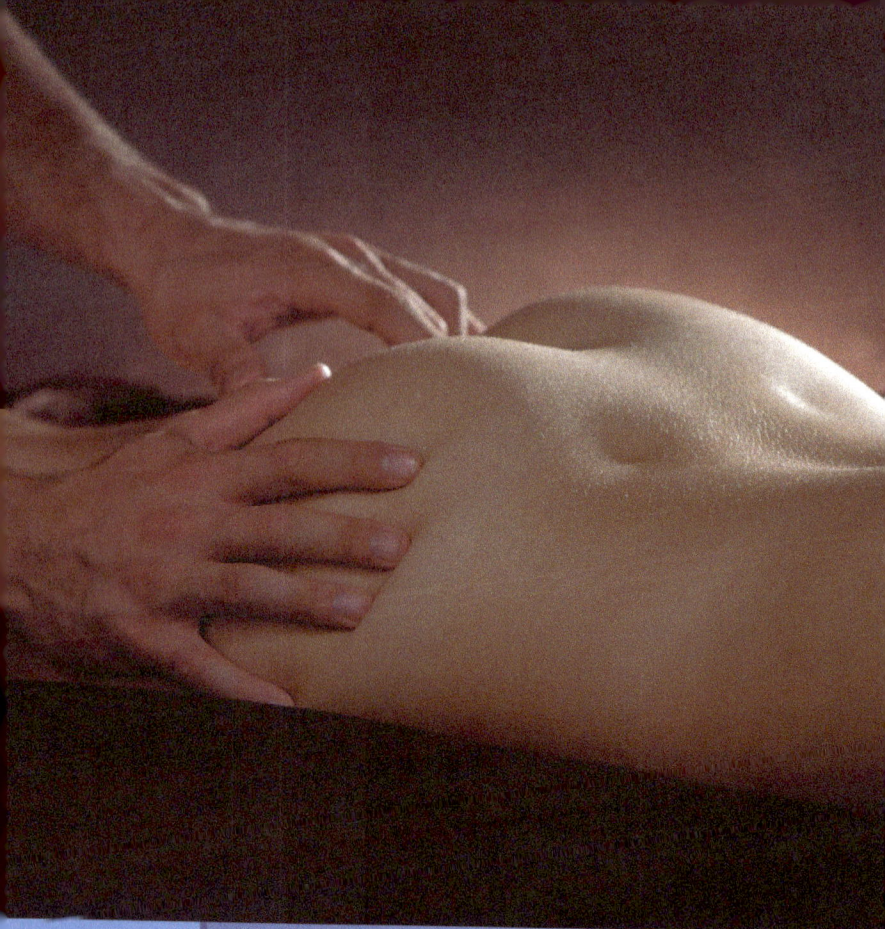

308 REAR WINDOW

He'll love the booty-full view of her curves, and she'll get lightheaded from the feeling of his hands caressing her sweet cheeks, dipping in and out of usually forbidden areas.

MASQUERADE 309

Pretending to be someone else completely changes the rules. Simply adding a mask to the sex ball lets lovers become more risqué and raunchy than they might be when just naked.

310 THE CATCHER

This high-energy, wide-open pose is bases loaded—he can sway his pine from side to side while she thrusts up and down and reaches between her legs to jerk one into the seats. Home run guaranteed!

TANTRIC OM | 311

Sitting and gazing into each other's eyes for a couple of minutes is harder than it sounds, but the payoff is a blissful bond so intimate and intense that nookie is almost beside the point.

312 NECK AND NECK

The neck is one of the hottest spots on her body that he can reach without removing a stitch of clothing. The skin here is so tender that a barely-there brush of the lips is enough to make her swoon.

DIRTY DANCING | 313

He can spend a few months working out to prepare for this pose, but using a wall will produce faster results. Even then, make sure there's a soft place for her to make a just-in-case crash landing.

314 UP IN ARMS

He'll earn big brownie points by expanding his focus and giving some lovin' to those neglected parts of her body during foreplay—like the thin skin on the inside of her arms.

SOFT SEDUCTION | 315

The art of seduction isn't about revealing all, but knowing just how much to reveal to make him want to see more.

316 SUCKING THE MANGO

The Kama Sutra features an entire chapter on fellatio. Here she takes him halfway in her mouth and sucks hard. When she feels he's about to boil over, she can advance to swallow whole and devour the rest of him.

HOT UNDER THE COLLAR | 317

There's something about an exposed neck that just cries out for a nibble and a suck.

318 LOVE TOKEN

For lovers going on a journey, making a "token of remembrance" on their thigh by pressing fingers into the skin to create three or four close lines will keep them yearning and burning until they return.

HANDY TOOL | 319

With woman-on-top, any kind of vibrator pressed against her adds a little extra zing. If she holds the tool, it'll leave his hands free for . . . other things.

320 BUTT YOGA

This pose seems relaxing, but it actually completely exposes him, allowing him to surrender to wherever her tongue probes.

THE SWING 321

Holding her arms means she can let go (trust game, anyone?) while he pulls against her push. The tandem back-and-forth will fire up the friction for an intense fallout (and collapse).

322 | TONGUE LAP

The tongue is highly charged with sexual chi, so instead of simply sucking his nipples, she should try lavishing them with lingering licks.

YOGA WHEELBARROW 323

She can show him how all that time in yoga class has paid off with this coming from behind move. They can turn this into sex on the run—literally—by trying to walk around the room while staying in position.

324 PRESSED POSITION

An all-around winner that produces excellent G-spot and multiple orgasms, gives his package a workout, and takes out the wash. Holding hands means he can pull her up and take some of the strain off her back. Awww.

REAR OFFICE | 325

Of course having sex on the work desk is cliché . . . but him rimming her rump is a complete power rush for her ("Please explain my spreadsheets while you're down there!").

326 LOCK UP

Once he has her in cuffs, he can start to kiss, nibble, suck, spank, tease, or even torture her with a vibrator to the point where she might beg him to take things to the next level—but there won't be a thing she can do about it.

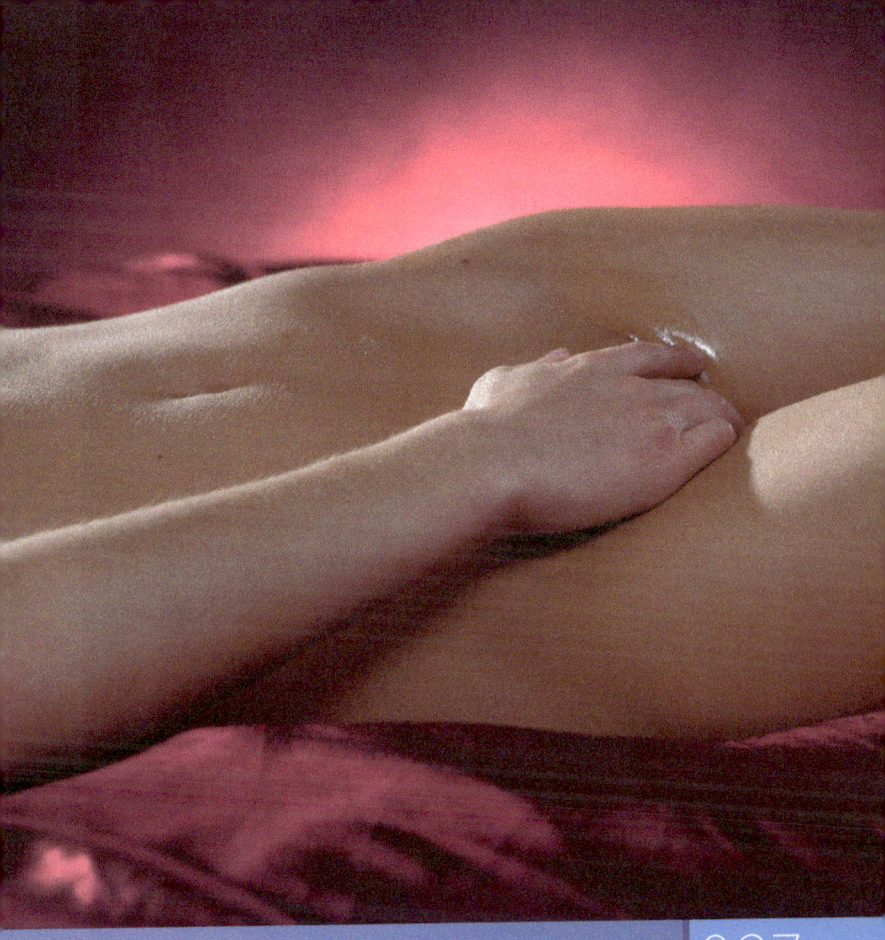

ELECTRIC SLIDE | 327

The best kind of carnal canoodling comes from friction, so less is more when using oil in love play. Warning: Latex and oil do not mix.

328 | TUM TUM

The stretch of flesh just below his belly button is a hot bed of tingly nerve endings practically hiding in plain sight—all she needs to do to turn him to mush is lightly drag her nails across the entire area.

SPOON RISE | 329

What's a girl to do when, upon waking, she feels his bits prodding her, except open wide on the side and say good morning? To keep the mood sexy sleepy, they can go slow and take minutes for what usually takes only seconds, savoring each stroke. Leave time for a shower.

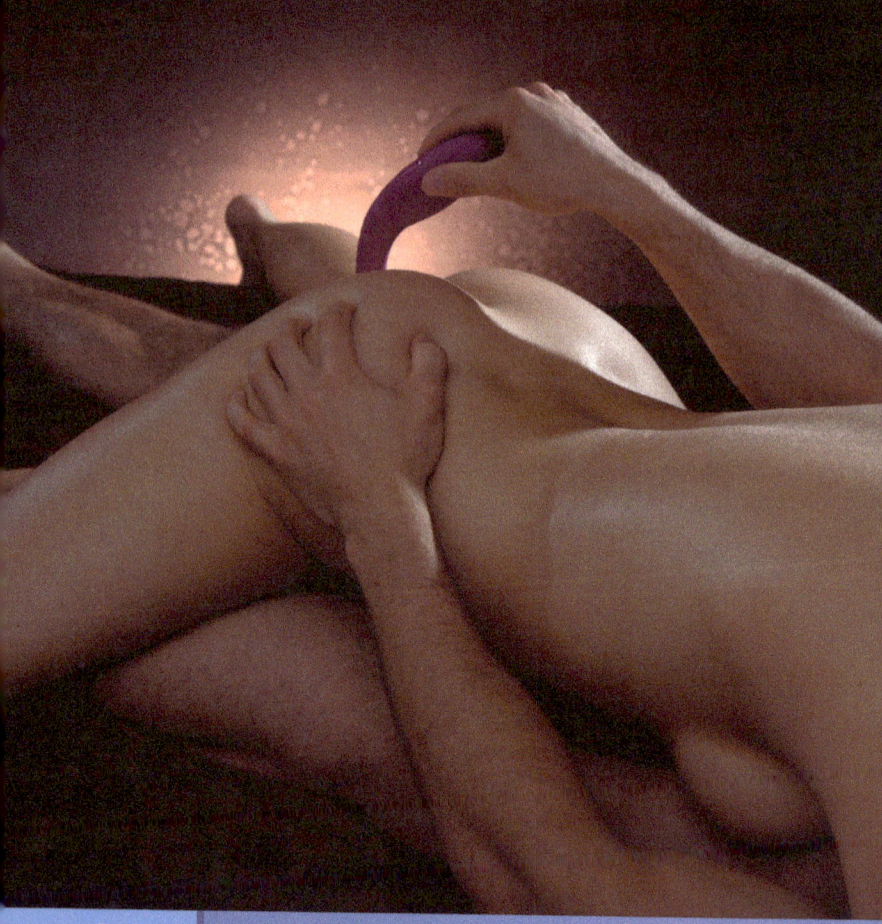

330 DOUBLE WHAM BAM

A vibrating anal buzz during sex makes for a delicious combo. But he'll need some sweet ambidextrous moves to continue to slide the toy in and out and all around while keeping up his end of the groin action.

ROCKING CHAIR | 331

No chair required—he provides the rock by swaying instead of thrusting with his hips. By semilifting her with one hand and stimulating her with the other, he'll send an all-points bulletin to her pleasure centers. A seat and a stimulator, who says men can't multitask?

332 FOREVER LOVE

An infinity symbol loops back and endlessly over itself. He can show his eternal connection to her by drawing it out over and over and—sigh—over again on her back, playing with pressure with each caress.

APHRODITE'S NECKLACE 333

Wrapping her legs around his neck so he can peer down between her parted legs will give their love play an almost mythical theme. Do expect thunderbolts.

334 PRESSURE DROP

A light stroke during massage might be too soothing if the aim is to get him in a relaxed state of mind for more horny high jinks later on. To keep him on his toes—and ready to curl them—mixing her caresses with some firm thumb presses along his back will fire up his system.

SHOW OFF | 335

This pose is not for the faint-of-heart . . . or leg. But once mastered, it does look spectacularly pornographic. She'll need to prop herself to avoid smothering him, as his mouth ministrations make her weak at the knees.

336 MIDNIGHT MASSAGE

With both their eyes closed, she lets her hands do the exploring—start with his strong shoulders and neck, then slide over his pecs and abs before working down toward a happy beginning.

SWAN SPORT | 337

Before there was cowgirl, there was the swan. The advantage is she has a few G-spot jiggy options from swinging her legs side to side over his to resting her feet on his thighs and working her hips up and down. He, meanwhile, can sit back and enjoy the hot scene.

338 COME TO YOUR SENSES

Touch, sight, taste, smell, and sound . . . all are tools that enhance foreplay. The response is even more intense when one sense is blocked. So closing eyes as they cuddle will help lovers become mindful of the feel of bodies touching, the sound of hearts beating, and the unique smell and taste of each other's skin.

IN THE REAR 339

The key to inserting a butt plug is to use lots and lots and lots of water-based lube, to go as slow as possible, and, once it's in, to leave it alone so it can do its job: fill up the anal cavity to create an intensely powerful and intensely satisfying orgasm.

340 BUTTRESS HIM UP

Spreading his cheeks will add tantalizing tension to her massage, especially if she finishes with a light tap on his perineum.

SHE'S THE COOK | 341

The woman doesn't always need to be lying on her back to receive oral sex. When she's sitting up, she has much more control over how quickly things heat up in her kitchen. Mmm. Delicious.

342 HITTING THE SPOT

This on-her-knees pose makes it easier for her to tickle her G-spot. The best tactic for insane pleasure is for her to bend her finger in a come-hither move and then use a gentle two-finger tapping motion against the fleshy knob on the front wall of her vajayjay.

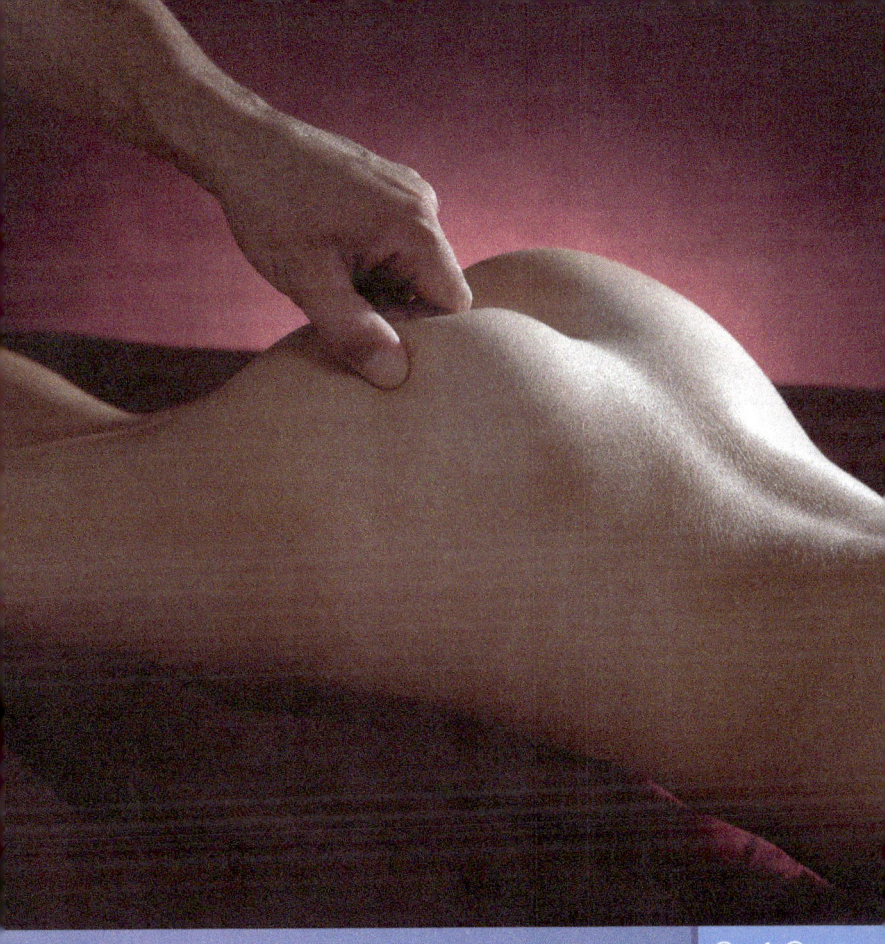

BUTT LOVE | 343

To hit just the right note between raunchy and rough play, he can take a leaf out of the Kama Sutra and pinch-hit the fleshy part of her rear with a series of hard love squeezes before flipping her over for the big finish.

344 ALL-DAY JOB

She'll want to make sure that her carnal calendar is cleared to take full advantage of his juicy work ethic.

FEATHERLIGHT | 345

The barely-there tickle of a feather up and down her body—but mostly focusing on her hot zones—is sure to produce a surprise sensation.

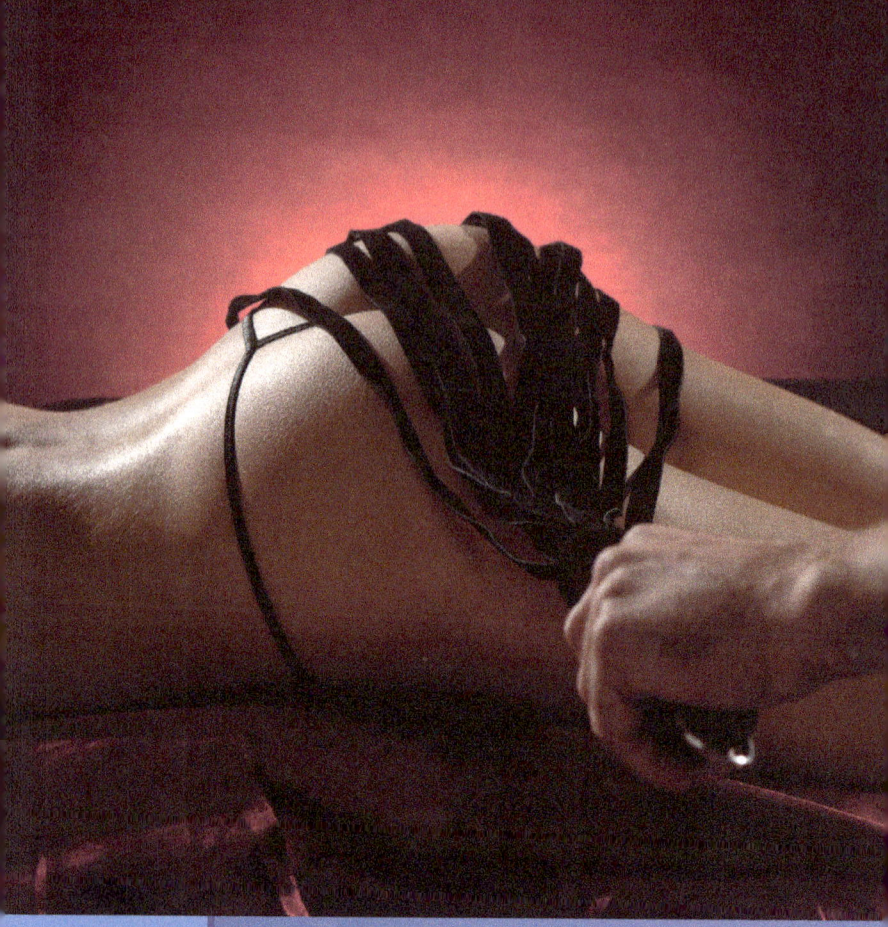

346 PURR-FECT PLAY

A leather whip is hard to beat when it comes to introducing an extra wow-factor to sex play. The rear end is loaded with sensitive nerve endings. Every cheeky thwack gets the blood flowing to the area, express delivering a sweet smack.

UPWARD MISSION 347

When the woman shifts the position of her legs and angle of her body, it turns basic missionary into an entirely new four-star pose. To add one more star, she can try rhythmically squeezing her PC muscles.

348 OVER EASY

So much attention focuses on the front of a woman's body, it's easy to forget that the back has a lot of touch-me-now nerve endings.

YES, MASTER 349

It's important to agree on a safe word to stop play before breaking out the floggers and binds. Also, couples should take turns being master and being dominated. Being in control can be heady, but surrender is sweet.

350 OMMM, OMMM, OHHHHHH!

When performing Tantra, it's important to be as centered and in the moment as possible to experience the highest ecstasy. To sync transcendentally, lovers can cuddle up, staring deep in each other's eyes as they try to harmonize their breathing to their bodies' movements.

GIVE HIM THE FINGER 351

A simple suck on his fingers while locking eyes is pure bliss.

352 THE NEWTON

Raising herself on all fours adds a gravitational pull to her pleasure as the blood flows down through her hanging breasts to her nipples, making them extrasensitive (and ripe for plucking).

MAN CHAIR | 353

Very little movement is required—or possible—here. But not a lot is needed, as the pleasure payoff comes from the bottomless penetration.

354 FOOTSIE FOREPLAY

The foot-sensation part of the brain is conveniently located right next to the genital region, so when she rubs down there, he mmm-mmm feels it up there.

PUCKER UP | 355

Anything that comes from the rear can sometimes feel too impersonal. When she wants something more intimate, she can turn her head and kiss and kiss and—sigh—kiss some more.

356 BOTTOM BOMBSHELL

What makes this move so delicious is the element of surprise—she can't really see him and has no idea what to expect.

HOT TO TROT | 357

Sucking the toe while biting it creates what's known in the Kama Sutra as a "swollen bite" of bliss—but what she'll call a do-me-now move.

358 KEEP ON ROCKING

Instead of moving her hips up and down to build up steam, she can simply rock them in languid loops, stirring up some luscious clitoral friction.

SPOON IT UP | 359

The entwining of their bodies means that most of the extracurricular movement is going to be above the belt. Most men can hold this pose for a long time without climaxing, making intercourse last far longer.

360 RUSH JOB

When the primal urge takes over and they have an amorous appointment they just have to keep, they can push all the clutter to the ground and use the desk in more—er—stimulating ways.

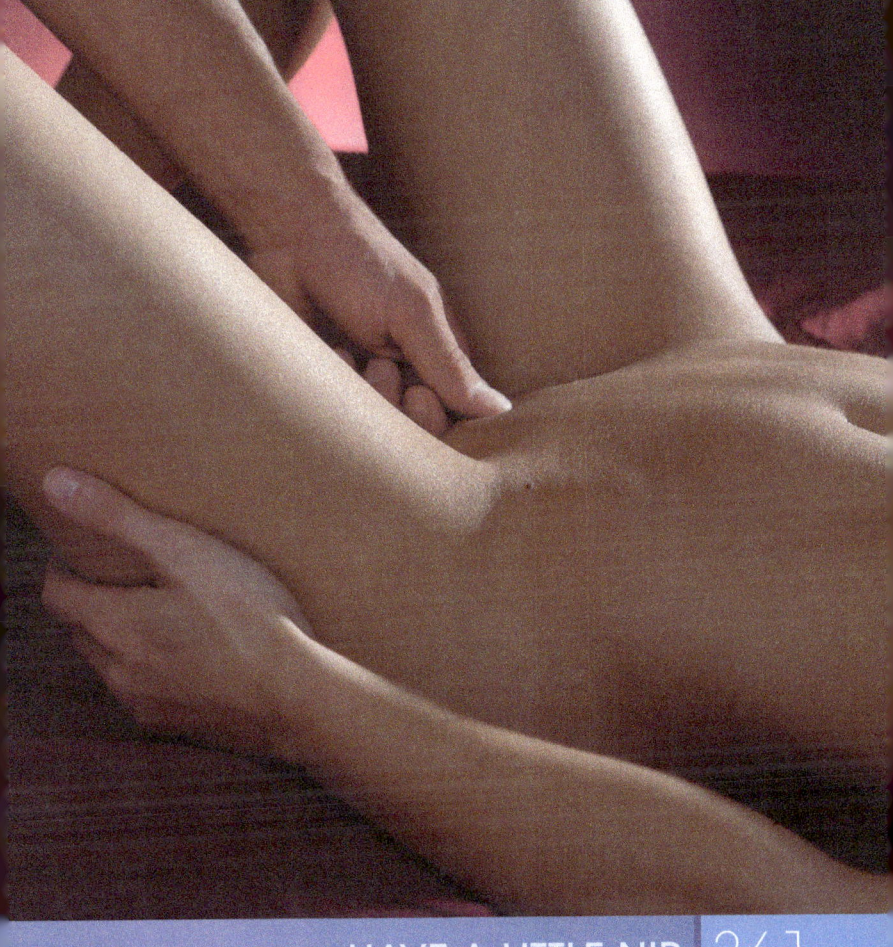

HAVE A LITTLE NIP 361

This part of her body can take a lot of hands-on stimulation, particularly once she's aroused. Using contrasting caresses such as pinches and pets, tugs and tickles, hard massages and soft strokes will keep her on her toes.

362 STRETCH IT OUT

Big, strong muscles may make a girl swoon, but this pose requires him to have lots of flexibility so his leg doesn't cramp at what could be an inopportune moment.

SKIRT FLIRT | 363

In romantic movies from the forties, all it took was the flash of a woman's calf to make a man weak at the knees.

364 SLIP AND SLIDE

The hot shock of warm, scented oil dripped on her body is sure to make her writhe with delight, especially when he uses soft, feather-light strokes to rub it over every inch of her body. The slow buildup will send shivers down her spine.

ROW HIS BOAT 365

This is one of the more difficult chair positions to master, but the deep penetration makes it worth it. The chef's tip is for her to lean back to get things moving. The possibility of a simultaneous orgasm is the cherry on the steamy sundae.

POSITIONS INDEX

A Light Touch, 242
A Thousand Kisses, 48
A Touch of Glass, 32
A Word in His Ear, 143
Ab-Solutely Ahhh!, 150
Ab-Solutely Fabulous, 226
Afternoon Delight, 259
All Bases Covered, 193
All Choked Up, 169
All-Day Job, 344
All Tied Up, 80
Anywhere BJ, 243
Aphrodite's Necklace, 333
The Arch, 222
Aural Love, 285
Backing It Up, 140
Backstroke, 254
Backward Bear, 263
Begging for More, 4
Belly Buddha, 42
Belly Up, 10
Bench Press Blow Job, 131
Bendy Spoon, 47
Best BJ, 24
Big Toe, 287
Bite It, 46
Bite Me, 278
Blind Date, 69
Blind Man's Bluff, 2
Bliss Buttons, 41
Blow the Man Down, 147
Blow-by-Blow, 302

Blue Plate Special, 229
Body Press, 265
Bonkarama Special, 284
Bottom Bombshell, 356
Bottom's Up, 74
Breast Is Best, 262
Buff It Up, 230
Bunny Hop, 271
Butt Love, 343
Butt Yoga, 320
Butter Up, 94
Buttress Him Up, 340
The Cappuccino, 166
Carnal Feast, 22
The Catcher, 310
Cheeky Girl, 67
Child's Pose, 209
Chill Out, 304
Chill Thrill, 11
Classic Twining, 120
Clean Sweep, 133
Climbing The Tree, 183
Close Shave, 86
Coffee Break, 136
Come to Your Senses, 338
Cook's Choice, 53
Cooked to Order, 219
Core Power, 153
Core-Gasm, 57
Corner Office, 217
Cowpoke, 207
Cozy Clasp, 261

Crossover, 215
Crow's Nest, 68
Cuddle Up, 199
Daily Grind, 253
Deep Impact, 116
Deep Throat, 103
Desk Duty, 132
Dirty Dancing, 313
Dirty Kisses, 56
Doggy on the Table, 93
Double Wham Bam, 330
Double Whammy, 190
Doubling Down, 238
Dress for Sex-Cess, 214
Dressing Down, 225
Drop by Drop, 61
Easy Grab, 276
Easy Rider, 205
Electric Slide, 327
Entwined Lovers, 141
Everything But . . . , 54
Extreme Intimate
  Makeover, 248
Feather Foreplay, 301
Featherlight, 345
Feed Your Face, 37
Finger Kiss, 14
Finger-Licking Good, 176
Flying High, 211
Foot Job, 88
Footsie Foreplay, 354
Forever Love, 332
Freestyle, 18
Frying His Corndog, 151
Full Throttle, 59

Fur-Tastic, 279
The G-Force, 95
G-Spot Feast, 300
Galloping Horse, 196
Game Night, 182
The Genie, 282
Get Wet, 220
Getting Cheeky, 75
Give Him a Hand, 198
Give Him the Finger, 351
Giving Lip, 60
Giving Pointers, 246
Good Lift, 228
Grindstone, 267
Hands-On, 111
Handy 69, 15
Handy on The Job, 212
Handy Tool, 319
Happy Buddha, 247
Have a Little Nip, 361
Head Honcho, 31
Head-On, 134
Headrest, 269
Helping Hand, 9
Her Mission, 26
Here, Doggy!, 256
High Five, 25
Hit the Trigger, 127
Hitting the Spot, 342
Hokeypokey, 231
Hold 'Em, 251
Honey Trap, 45
Hot Hands, 175
Hot To Trot, 357
Hot Under the Collar, 317

367

Humpty Bumpty, 274
Hurts So Good, 34
Ignition Switch, 148
In His Face, 206
In His Head, 62
In Sync, 70
In the Deep, 171
In the Hot Seat, 224
In the Rear, 339
Intensified Play, 257
Intimate Things, 8
Joystick, 296
Jump Start, 185
Jungle Fever, 249
Keep Him on His Toes, 117
Keep on Rocking, 358
Keep Your Hands to Yourself, 123
Kiss Your Miss, 165
Kiss-Off, 108
Kissing the Yoni, 173
Kitchen Encounter, 264
Kneel and Deliver, 121
Knees Up, 163
La Cage aux Folles, 1
Ladies and Gents, 234
Lady's Squeeze, 216
Lap Dance, 179
Lap It Up, 203
Lazy-Boy, 58
Lazy-Girl, 188
Let It Slide, 258
Lie Back and Enjoy, 159
Lift Up, 77
Liftoff, 51

Light Duties, 178
The Lioness, 187
Little Minx, 44
Little Piggies, 126
Lock Up, 326
Look, Do Touch, 194
The Lotus, 288
Love at First Bite, 21
Love Bites, 73
Love Token, 318
Lover's Gaze, 236
Lover's Porn, 152
Lunar Launch, 252
Lusty Livelihood, 299
Lying Wheelbarrow, 227
Magic Mirror, 202
Magic Touch, 172
Make Your Mark, 162
Man Chair, 353
Man on a Mission, 109
Masquerade, 309
Ménage à Two and a Half, 12
Midnight Massage, 336
Milk and Water Embrace, 142
The Mind-Bender, 135
Mindless Work, 66
Mirror, Mirror on the Wall, 89
Mounting of the Ass, 233
Mounting on the Ball, 292
Moving Mountains, 101
Mystery Lover, 119
Nail Art, 106
Nail Him, 87

Naked Spooning, 239
The Nautilus, 170
Naughty Nurse, 145
Navel-Gazing, 114
Neck and Neck, 312
Negligent Foreplay, 28
New Necking, 232
The Newton, 352
Nip Tips, 291
Oeufs de l'Extase, 3
Office Oral, 189
Office Space, 97
Olympic Orgasms, 177
Ommm, Ommm, Ohhhhhh!, 350
On His Knees, 160
On the Bench, 90
On the Mound, 204
On the Side, 115
On the Waterfront, 181
On Top Is Tops, 293
Once Bitten, 113
Open for Business, 297
Oral Buzz, 208
Over Easy, 348
Pay Lip Service, 99
Peeling and Revealing, 105
Peep Show, 65
Pet the Pooch, 146
Picture Perfect, 91
The Pinner, 63
Plat du Jour, 71
Play Ball, 19
Playing Hot and Cold, 266
Playing Rough, 305
The Plow, 63
Plump It Up, 78
Pose With a View, 277
Posterior Pickup, 118
Prasarita, 200
Pressed Position, 324
Pressure Drop, 334
Pressure Points, 29
Pucker Up, 355
Pull It Off, 290
Pull the Pony, 223
Puppy Love, 124
Purr-Fect Play, 346
The Push, 174
Ramp It Up, 36
Rear Office, 325
Rear Window, 308
The Reclining Chair, 16
Relax and Release, 130
Reverse Spoon, 39
Ride Him Hard, 92
Rise to Crescendo, 149
Rising Position, 213
Rocking Chair, 331
Rosebud, 158
Row His Boat, 365
Rub a Dub Dub, 164
Rush Job, 360
Sacred Sacrum, 191
Saddle Up, 100
Satisfaction Guaranteed, 104
Seamless Kiss, 125
Seated Wheelbarrow, 281
Secret Rapture, 72

369

Secret Rush, 192
Seed with Rice, 294
Sexy Spoon, 218
Sexy Topping, 186
Shake and Bake, 245
She's the Cook, 341
Sheer Delight, 195
Shotgun, 98
Show Off, 335
Show Your Tongs, 85
Shower Your Senses, 139
Sitting Pretty, 110
68, 154
68 Redux, 144
Skirt Flirt, 363
The Skype Is the Limit, 273
Slick Strokes, 138
Slide, Baby, Slide, 255
Slip and Slide, 364
Slow Strip, 167
Snuggly, 122
Soap on a Rope, 13
Soft Seduction, 315
Soixante-Neuf, 137
South Seas Rock, 43
Space Shuttle, 7
Speaking Greek, 221
Special Tonight, 286
Speed Bumps, 107
The Sphinx, 30
Spin the Top, 55
Spiral, 64
Splitting the Bamboo, 33
Spoon It Up, 359
Spoon Rise, 329

Stand Tall, 129
Starfish, 168
Steam Up, 283
Stocking Filler, 84
Straddle Cuddle, 184
Stretch It Out, 362
Sucking the Mango, 316
Sunday Hammock, 102
Supported Bridge, 280
Swan Sport, 337
The Swing, 321
Switch-Hit, 303
Tailgating, 156
Tainted Love, 244
Take a Position, 155
Take Charge, 272
Take It Off, 6
Tantric Om, 311
Tasty Toe, 275
Teasing Strip, 112
Teasing Touches, 23
Tender Moments, 260
Tender Touch, 157
Thigh Sigh, 270
Thrusters, 17
Tic Toc, Tic Toc, 50
Tight End, 83
Tipping Point, 161
Toe Job, 20
Tomcat, 27
Tongue Lap, 322
Tongue Tickles, 241
Tooled for Fun, 82
Tootsie Treat, 128
Top and Tail, 237

Top Secret Touch, 76
Topping the Table, 307
Torrid Tutorial, 180
Treasure Chest, 40
Tress Tease, 96
Tug-of-War, 306
Tum Tum, 328
Twisted T, 240
U Go, Girl!, 197
Under Pressure, 201
Up Close and Personal, 81
Up in Arms, 314
Up in Arms, 52
Upward Mission, 347
Va-Va-Voom, 35
Virtual Fun, 289
Wake-Up Call, 210
Wash Behind the Ears, 38
Who's the Boss?, 79
The Windsor, 49
Woman on a Mission, 295
Woman's Best Friend, 250
The Wrap-Up, 268
The Yawning, 298
Yee-Haw!, 235
Yes, Master, 349
Yoga Wheelbarrow, 323

ABOUT THE AUTHOR

Lisa Sweet is the author of numerous sexual instruction books and has had her writing published in newspapers and magazines in the United States, the United Kingdom, France and Australia.

www.ingramcontent.com/pod-product-compliance
Lightning Source LLC
Chambersburg PA
CBHW041732300426
44116CB00018B/2954